"Success" vs. Success

The Game of a Lifetime

9 Lessons for young athletes
(and everybody else)
to achieve real success
in sports, career, family, and life

D1048047

Written by RICK POPP

October 1, 2020.

Copyright © 2020 Rick Popp.

In loving memory of my brother Tim

CONTENTS

Introduction

In the summer of 2019, I had just retired from a nearly 30-year career in human resources at a Fortune 15 company, had recently sold my home near the corporate headquarters, and moved back near my rural hometown in the upper peninsula of Michigan to begin the next chapter of my life. So when a former college football teammate of mine, who now coaches football at a small high school near my hometown, asked me to speak to a group of about 200 high school football players at a local football camp, I found myself intrigued and challenged to take my life experiences and come up with something of value for young people to learn and take with them in an impactful way.

That simple request to speak was the impetus for a reflective journey of mine, fresh from retiring from an intense corporate career and a desire to especially help young people early in their own journeys that has resulted in me writing this book. Here's my story and why I believe that this book will add value to you and/or to your players, children, or friends in order to lead a more fulfilling, rewarding, joyful, successful life — in athletics, working career, and family.

I set out to write this book for young people, especially those playing youth, high school, or college sports, and recently graduated student-athletes. At that time, I also knew that all former athletes would be able to draw from their past experiences as athletes and apply what was planted deep inside their character during that special phase of their lives. And I had no doubt that I was also writing this for parents, coaches, teachers, and other mentors who may read this book in order to assist young people, especially young athletes, as they coach and teach our youth to achieve their full potential in sports, and more importantly to take full advantage of their sports experiences to help enable them to lead fulfilling, successful lives.

But after hearing back from the first readers of the draft of this book, it became clear that I have written for an audience well beyond young athletes and their supporters. If you are neither a young person, athlete, former athlete, mentor, parent, teacher, nor a coach, and are looking for tips to career and family success, read on! Although the target audience for this book is young athletes and their key supporters, **I believe the advice given applies to anybody for their work career and family lives.** Whether you learn these lessons via athletics, robotics, being in a band, project team, working in a job with a team, or any form of team or competitive experience, I am confident that the lessons shared in this book will help you too. That said, because of my initial target audience, you'll see and hopefully enjoy many sports analogies, stories, and quotes from famous athletes along the way.

Good Start, Take The Time You Need, and Finish!

Regardless of your background, **I applaud you for making the decision to get better**, to grow as an athlete, to set yourself up to be a more successful professional, and to be an even better family person. **I challenge you to not only start this book, but finish it.** Take your time, read a bit at a time, perhaps one key lesson per day, but keep going until the end. If you get tired or distracted from reading, put this book down for a while, go for a run, get a snack, take a nap, do some push-ups, or whatever you need to do, then come back, maybe the next day, and pick up where you left off. Set a schedule for reading if that will help you stick to it. But **commit to finishing it and finish it relatively soon.** If you make this commitment, **I'm 100% confident that it will be worth your time and you will be on a path to greater success.**

With that, I hope you enjoy this book and take away something that will make a significant impact in the rest of your life, starting *today*.

My Journey to Learning These Lessons

Before I get into the 9 Lessons, allow me to share a little background on my own journey, which led to my discovering the life lessons explained in this book.

Like many of you, athletics were a huge part of my young life. At that time, when I was at a football camp, basketball practice, tennis tournament, or baseball field, just like many of you for hours and hours every week, I knew that I was learning and growing as an athlete and as a person. However, I did not realize how significantly the life lessons I was learning that very day, that camp, that practice, that game, that season would apply to the rest of my athletic career, even more so to my professional career, and most importantly to my family life. That is precisely what I am writing to you about — *to be aware of and apply the lessons you have already learned and are learning to your remaining football, basketball, baseball, tennis, volleyball,…whatever your chosen endeavor, then do the same to your future jobs and professional careers, and at the same time apply them to your family life. Use what you learn in your athletic experience to succeed in the game of your life - the game of a lifetime.*

Note: As I mentioned in the introduction, these lessons apply to non-athletes as well, those who have chosen a different path of being challenged to develop skills and achieve success.

Likewise, these lessons relate to every age, not only to young people.

Establishing Credibility

At the risk of appearing to "toot my own horn," I need to establish at least some credibility with you before I get into sharing tips and advice to achieving success and finding fulfillment and joy in athletics, careers, and in your family. Certainly, many people are more accomplished than me, yet I know I have been fortunate to have successes in my life, in athletics, in my career, and in my family. And before you listen to any of my advice, I assume you'd like to know why I think I may have something to offer, especially on matters as important as your personal fulfillment and joy. So allow me to share a bit more about my background and experiences that give me confidence in writing this book for you and will hopefully give you a sense of confidence in me as your advisor in this book.

Athletics Journey

I was blessed to be raised in Iron Mountain, a small town in the Upper Peninsula of Michigan, known for being the site of one of Ford Motor Company's earliest factories, the home of the World's Highest Ski Jump, and more recently famous for being the hometown of Hall of Fame Michigan State basketball coach Tom Izzo and former NFL and collegiate football head coach and NFL Network Analyst Steve Mariucci, two of my earliest and life-long role-models. Like coaches Izzo and Mariucci, I was gifted with some athletic and leadership abilities, but more importantly we were all blessed with hall of fame coaches, outstanding teammates and friends, a supportive community, and a wonderful families with loving parents and siblings.

In high school in my day, the Iron Mountain Mountaineers were dominant in our region in the Upper Peninsula of Michigan. I was the point guard in basketball, the quarterback in football, played both doubles and singles in tennis, and played second base and catcher in baseball. In my junior year of high school, my team won every football game of the regular season and in the first round of the state playoffs (10-0), until losing in the state semi-finals by a field goal in the final seconds of the game. That same year, we won every basketball game (24-0), until losing in the state quarterfinals. My tennis doubles partner and I won every tennis set and match that season to win my third of three doubles tennis championships in the Upper Peninsula of Michigan. In my senior year of high school, the success continued, though with only a few blemishes. We had championship teams in every sport and I was a proud captain of my teams. Several of my former high school teammates went on to have fantastic athletic careers and professional success, including Todd Penegor, CEO of Wendy's, who makes a few appearances later in this book.

Following high school, I received a full scholarship to play quarterback at Northern Michigan University. After sitting the bench for a couple years, I eventually became a team captain and starting quarterback as a junior and senior. In my senior year, the NMU football Wildcats became the undefeated Great Lakes Intercollegiate Athletic Conference champions, and lost only one game to a non-conference opponent that year. We were the country's top-ranked NCAA Division II football team for several weeks and ultimately lost in the NCAA DII national semi-finals in a close game. I was privileged to be part of that team, the best team of my athletic career, and was also honored to be recognized as All-Conference, All-American, and team most valuable player, and years later was inducted into the NMU Sports Hall of Fame.

Professional Career Journey

As my days of participating in competitive athletics came to an end, I was quite clueless about anything outside of sports. I had good grades in high school and in my undergraduate studies in college, but had little work experience and limited work skills and knowledge outside of the sports for which I was so passionate. You may have had or will have the same "clueless" feeling and nervousness about what you will be doing after sports (or after college, or after your current job). But that's ok, it's a common feeling.

Fortunately, my athletics experiences, development, and exposure gave me opportunities that I didn't totally appreciate until later in my life. After college, my resume and credentials were just enough to land a job with the Ford Motor Company. And as I began to get comfortable with the actual job I was hired to do, I could see how my preparation and development through athletics was a tremendous help to me. And after nearly 30 years working in that fantastic company, after 15 different positions and 9 promotions, I retired as an executive director of human resources, where I served hundreds of thousands of employees, retirees, and their families. In addition, I participated on multiple boards of directors and leadership teams outside of my main jobs. Now, I manage my own consulting business where I help leaders, teams, organizations, and companies unleash their potential for more success.

In other words, much of my 30-year work career has been focused on developing successful professionals and successful teams in the workplace, across multiple types of work, products, countries, and cultures.

But beyond my own professional experience and success is the fact that I've had a front row seat for many years in witnessing some of the most successful business people in the world, some with whom I had the opportunity to work directly as a business partner and close confidant, and others for whom I was a part of their broader team. Much of my viewpoint regarding the underlying reasons for success and failure have come from working closely with or for these special leaders.

Family Journey

And with most pride, for the past 30 years, I have had the honor and blessing to be married to a magnificent woman, my wife Sue. She is beautiful both inside and out and I am as in-love with her today as the day that I asked her to marry me. We have become a strong team as spouses and parents in leading our family. Like me, Sue was also influenced greatly by athletics in her life, career, and with our family. She was a high school and college basketball standout, played collegiate basketball on an athletic scholarship, captained her teams and had post-season playoff success herself. Later, she worked in banking and office administration for several years before becoming a PGA golf professional.

Together, Sue and I have raised two amazing sons, Sam and Isaiah, who continue to make us proud for the young men they have become. Sam and Isaiah have also had their share of successes and failures in high school, club, and collegiate athletics, Sam primarily in soccer and Isaiah mainly in football. Guiding them and learning from them through their own achievements, failures, and challenges in their athletics, education, and early professional career has also enhanced my growth as a leader and parent. My family is the most important and the most successful team that I've been a part of in my life. That is why I'm so passionate about the advice in this book pertaining to family as well as career and athletics.

Again, please forgive me for "tooting my own horn" in this section. I only tell you my journey to establish a certain level of credibility before giving you advice. And as important as my own personal experience is the fact that I've played with, worked with, and lived with many successful people for over 50 years. My journey and observations include all of them.

How Do We Define Success?

Tis is a profound question that can, and does, have many different answers, depending on who you ask and depending on the circumstances of a given time, team, or purpose. I have already used the term "success" many times in the first few pages of this book — three times on the book cover alone — and you may be starting to wonder what I mean by "success." I'll explore the definition of success more deeply later in this book. My personal journey includes a lifetime of defining and redefining what success means in this world and what real success means — to others and to me.

For now, keep the definition of success simply as "the accomplishment of an aim or purpose." A successful person, therefore, is one who has been able to accomplish their aim or purpose with a certain level of consistency, although periodic failures are certainly a part of every successful journey.

In athletics, we can quite easily expect that many people aim to, for example, play to the best of their abilities, earn a starting position, come together as a team to beat a strong opponent or rival, have a winning season, or winning a conference title, a state, or national championship, perhaps even an Olympic gold medal for the elite few in the world. For some of the top teams, nothing short of a championship is considered success, while other teams that are new or rebuilding may make their aim or purpose to be a winning season (winning more games than losing) for that particular year to be considered a success. We can normally consider post-season honors, like all-conference, all-sate, or most valuable player, as individual success within a team environment.

Professional or career success can be identified in general as doing one's job well, achieving the desired results of a particular position, being viewed as a valued member of the work team, being recognized for expertise and job knowledge, receiving excellent performance reviews, perhaps even professional awards and distinguished forms of formal recognition for a certain level of expertise or particular accomplishment. Career goals often include continually growing levels of responsibilities, promotions to bigger jobs, and higher levels of pay and special benefits or perks. Society often views the most successful business people or other professionals as those who are most well-known or who have been able to achieve high levels of wealth.

In families, parents quite naturally aim to ensure their family members do well in school, jobs, music, art, sports, ... whatever activities they choose. Moreover, many successful families strive to achieve a tight unit where each cares deeply for each other, supports and sacrifices for each other, and where each family member makes the effort to help the family stay together and continually grow stronger as a family unit.

In each of these venues (sports, career, and family), evidence such as mentioned above can suggest that the aim or purpose of the sport, the job/career, and the family are being accomplished.

And yet, "success" can be confusing and elusive; its definition is not always clear. "Success" for one person may not be success for another. Who is the final judge of success anyway?

Despite the potential complications of defining success, at least for now, we'll use the simple definition mentioned earlier this paragraph, "the accomplishment of an aim or purpose," but we will later explore an even deeper perspective of "success." Whatever you choose to do in your life, it is noble and appropriate to strive to be successful in that part of your life. This book is intended to help you do that, no matter how you personally define success.

Observations of Successful Teams and Individuals

So with that bit of my personal background during these past four decades, along with a brief reflection of what we mean by "success," I have been a part of, led, and/or have worked with tens of thousands of people, and hundreds of teams looking to achieve success. I have experienced personal success _and failures_ and have seen close-up many more successes and failures of countless other individuals, teams, families, and organizations.

With all of these years and experiences behind me, I'm going to share with you _9 Lessons_ and a few additional thoughts, based on my personal experience, expertise, and observations, on what you are learning right now in your football camp, at your volleyball practices, on your basketball team, on the sheet in hockey or the pitch in soccer, or whichever sport you are playing, that I guarantee will give you even more _success, including a deeper fulfillment, and more joy and happiness_ in:

1) Your sport(s)

2) Your jobs and career

3) Your family

I have learned these lessons by having experienced much success, but also by making many mistakes and experiencing failure; and, once again, I've observed others do the same for half of a century.

Throughout this book, I share quotes from many thoughts leaders and role models; athletes, presidents, business leaders, scientists, and others who are considered as some of the most successful people today and in history from around the world. They lived most or all of these lessons in rising to their levels of success and they also had their own share of mistakes. So we learn both from others successes and failures, as Eleanor Roosevelt, US diplomat & reformer and wife of President Franklin Roosevelt, once said, "Learn from the mistakes of others. You can't live long enough to make them all yourself."

Watch the Entire Movie!

I again encourage you to commit to reading this entire book. The further you go, the more you'll get out of it and the more you'll get out of the best part at the end. Just like when you're watching a movie, the end depends on the entire movie and the best endings are when they connect back through the full storyline. The same for this book.

Each lesson can stand on its own, but each is maximized when considered in conjunction with the others, and the full impact hinges on the final link of the chain at the end. Then, after you've gotten through the entire book, you can use the 9 individual lessons by themselves as reference in the future.

So let's go!

Lesson #1: Be Coachable

Although these 9 Lessons aren't all in a particular order, this one is intentionally first — **Be Coachable**.

Being Coachable in Athletics

You are blessed with having coaches right now, coaches who care about your success. And if you're lucky, you'll have a coach or two that ride you a bit harder than you may like. You may be angry about a coach getting angry with you, not giving you enough playing time, pointing out what you're doing wrong more than highlighting when you're doing something right, or pushing your buttons some other way. You may even be lucky enough to have a coach that you might think doesn't know too much about you or even the sport you play. Why do I say that is lucky? Because this will force you to think hard about being coachable. It is especially hard at times to hear critical feedback from a coach who you may think doesn't care about you or you may believe doesn't know as much about the sport as you may think they should. For when you have a coach, especially a tough coach, being coachable enables you to break through the anger, the discomfort, the desire to criticize the coach, and truly hear what that coach is telling you. Even a bad coach may be showing you something that will help you. But if you're not coachable, you won't see or hear the helpful advice through the noise that makes you un-coachable - your focus is not on the coaching, but on the coach.

Coaching the Fastest Human in the World

I like to use this example when talking about the times when we doubt the qualifications of a coach. Usain Bolt - the fastest human ever clocked in the 100 meter and 200 meter dashes, winner of 8 Olympic and 11 World Championship gold medals — had a coach by the name of Glen Mills. Did Glen Mills ever run as fast as Usain? Certainly not. Can Usain Bolt have taken the position that nobody could really help him because he was the best there had ever been in the 100 meter and 200 meter dashes? Sure, he could have taken that position. But does the fact that Usain's coach had never done what his athlete had done mean he could not help Usain shave another 0.01 off of a world record? Not at all. Usain's coach could, and did, provide a different perspective, a different set of eyes, critical analysis, knowledge of training, and offered potential solutions and direction for Usain to get even faster. When Usain's coach pointed out the slightest opportunity to get faster, do you think Usain took that advice or criticism as being too hard, as not recognizing all of Usain's success to date, as ignoring the world records that Bolt held at that time? Of course not. The coaching, the critical feedback, and the times of tough love were intended for Usain to simply get better and in no way disregarded or disrespected all the accomplishments and talent that was already there, including the world records.

To take this example further, after Bolt retired from competitive track, a few other sprinters were criticizing Glen

Mills as their coach and were moving to different coaches. When interviewed by a reporter in his homeland of Jamaica, Bolt defended the athletes' right to change coaches, but he more firmly defended his coach in the midst of the criticism from the other sprinters. As stated in an article from July 2019:

> *Bolt, who underlined that he has no issue with an athlete deciding to change coaches if they see this as the best decision for their careers, says he is deeply bothered by the lack of respect being shown towards Mills and believes athletes should take greater responsibility for their own failures.*

> *"You can leave a coach, I have moved on from coaches, but I didn't disrespect anybody. We parted ways because of differences that we had but when you are going to try and disrespect a coach – a coach that took you to a level that no one else did. It hurts me personally because it is my coach, and I know he won't be happy I am defending him like this, but these athletes should know themselves and respect that Glen Mills took them to the highest level they have ever been - they probably won't get back to that level, but he brought you there!" Bolt stated.[1]*

It is easy to blame a coach for lack of achievement. It's especially easy when you see flaws in your coach. But in the end, when you are coachable, you realize that the ultimate responsibility for your performance lies squarely within you.

---

[1]Jamaican news publication 'The Gleaner' from July 9, 2019 entitled, "Bolt Defends Former Coach Glen Mills Amid Criticism,"

Coaching is not about the Coach

Former NBA basketball coach George Karl, who is one of only 9 coaches in NBA history to have won 1,000 NBA games put it this way, "Who is the ally of the coach? Who's going to write, 'Man, that was a well-coached game.' Players win, coaches lose."

Being coachable is about you, not about your coach. Your coach will provide you advice and direction with which you'll decide what to do. Often, you'll agree immediately that the coach is right on with the advice. At times, you may not so readily agree. Being coachable is accepting your coach as a valuable source of advice and accepting that advice graciously and appreciably. You still own the responsibility and the ability to do what is best with that advice.

Michael Jordan's Best Skill

All-time basketball great Michael Jordan earned six NBA Finals Most Valuable Player (MVP) Awards, ten scoring titles (both all-time records), five MVP Awards, ten All-NBA First Team designations, nine All-Defensive First Team honors, fourteen NBA All-Star Game selections, three All-Star Game MVP Awards, three steals titles, and the 1988 NBA Defensive Player of the Year Award. He holds the NBA records for highest career regular season scoring average (30.12 points per game) and highest career playoff scoring average (33.45 points per game). In 1999, he was named the greatest North American athlete of the 20th century by ESPN, and was second to Babe Ruth on the Associated Press' list of athletes of the century. Jordan is a two-time inductee into the

Naismith Memorial Basketball Hall of Fame, having been enshrined in 2009 for his individual career and again in 2010 as part of the group induction of the 1992 United States men's Olympic basketball team (The Dream Team). And in light of all of that, Michael Jordan has said:

"My best skill was that I was coachable.
I was a sponge and aggressive to learn."

The Head Coach Book

Former NFL Head Coach and current NFL Network Analyst Steve Mariucci told me about how he prepared to become a head coach. Back when he was an assistant coach, including when he was the quarterback coach at the Green Bay Packers with the young and eventual Hall-of-Famer Brett Favre, he built a Head Coach Book. In it, he put everything that he thought he might need if he ever had the chance to become a head coach in the NFL. The book included practice plans, meeting schedules, the approach to the NFL draft, ... everything. He included his philosophy of coaching, which was developed through his years of coaching in college both as an assistant and head coach. He drew from his own experiences and what he "learned from everyone" with whom he worked and played for during his coaching career and his own playing days. He was constantly learning and thinking about how he could become a better coach. He built his Head Coach Book for that day, the if-I-ever-get-the-chance-to-be-an-NFL-head-coach day. And on that day when the San Francisco 49ers came to him at the young age of 42, he was ready to become a head coach in the National Football League.

Appreciate the Good and Bad

As I look back at my own less decorated athletic career than the greats that I mention in this book, I'd say I was quite coachable throughout my athletic experience. However, I was not always consistently coachable to the degree I could have been and to the degree that I'm recommending to you in this lesson.

For example, I remember my college quarterback coach, Mark Marana, during one of our many film sessions (yes, we used to watch "film" instead of YouTube or Hudl back then). Normally, film sessions would focus on what didn't go right and where improvements need to be made. As a quarterback, I always had opportunities to get better. In this particular session, as we were reviewing a series of sprint-out pass plays, plays where the quarterback sprints to one side or the other and throws the ball while on the run, Coach Marana tried to give me positive, encouraging feedback, saying, "Ricky, you roll out and throw to your left better than anybody I've seen." Wow, positive feedback from a football coach. Nice to hear! But instead of taking the compliment as I should have, graciously, appreciatively, and in a way that would continue to build a relationship between coach and player, and in a way that would encourage more feedback in the future (positive or negative), I replied, "What, is there something wrong with the way I roll and throw to the right?" Ugh. Opportunity blown. This is not being coachable, especially considering that it was positive feedback. One of my fellow quarterback buddies chuckled and shook his head, which made me realize how poorly my comment had come off. Coach Marana also gave an incredulous look, which made me realize my mistake. But then, to make matters worse, I tried to justify that I was simply making sure that there was no issue with me rolling to the right, yet trying to justify my reaction only dug a deeper hole. Even if my intentions were noble, if I truly was trying to be such a perfectionist that I wanted to focus on where I was weak, my reaction and comment only took away from my coachability. Further, my reaction raised the question for my coach — if I could not take positive feedback, how was I going to accept feedback of a more critical nature? How willing would coach be to challenge me with tough messages in the future? The good news is that my coach knew me well enough and kept coaching me, and I recognized that moment and remember that incident to this day. It helped me be more careful with accepting feedback, good or bad, which in turn built stronger relationships with coaches and teammates — ultimately improving my own performance and making the team stronger.

When a coach or teacher stops challenging you, stops providing feedback of a critical nature, he or she has given up on you. You are on your own. It's not where you ever want to be.

That all said, throughout my athletic experience, which included a several tough but great coaches, especially in football, and in observing other athletes and coaches during that time, I was able to build a solid foundation of being coachable, which I found to be extremely valuable in my business career.

Being Coachable in the Workplace

After my college football career ended, I had a brief assignment as a student assistant football coach, and then finished graduate school. I recall getting my first "real job" in an office environment at an automotive manufacturing plant that built car engines and fuel tanks. It was a new world for me, but one that I enjoyed thoroughly. It wasn't long that I recognized how valuable it was to have had the experience of being coached for several years in athletics.

Over nearly 30 years working with all types of employees in the workplace, *I can't tell you how many people that I have witnessed in the workplace that have trouble being coached.* Especially when I first came into the workforce from my athletics background, I was surprised to see how many people who had rarely or had never been given direct feedback of a critical nature and, when coaching came to them in the workplace in a way that suggested they could do better, it would throw them off rather than help as intended. Instead of viewing feedback as normal, as a gift, and an opportunity to get better, they would be stunned, take offense, blame, explain, or get overly emotional toward themselves or with the person giving the feedback. *So instead of growing from the feedback, they got worse.*

Employers want employees who are coachable. Athletes have had the chance to be coached and most have grown to appreciate being coached, they like to be coached, they expect to be coached. It is an advantage over other job candidates and employees looking for advancement.

In my early days in the workforce, when I was fresh from the classroom and the football field, and being used to having tough coaches, I remember having long conversations (or more like listening sessions) with my work colleagues about what our supervisor recently said, what s/he may have meant, why the supervisor was not right in saying what s/he said, what the supervisor should be doing differently, and so on.

I also saw people struggle accepting feedback even of a positive, complimentary nature. Instead of graciously accepting the "pat on the back," they awkwardly attempted to deflect, downplay, or explain away their moment of success or appreciation.

As I grew into leadership positions, I became responsible for the performance of increasingly larger teams with increased financial, human, and geographical responsibilities. So I was continually providing feedback to more and more people from different cultures with more complex operations. At the same time, I too was getting performance feedback from more senior levels of the company - the stakes were continually getting higher and the pressure to deliver results was even greater with each promotion. But the fundamentals of coaching and being coachable remained the same at all levels. I'll cover those a bit later in this lesson.

Warning: We are human. You would think that after having a lifetime of coaching myself, both on the receiving and giving sides of coaching, then having a career that deeply involves coaching, that I would always be coachable myself. Well, guess what, I too would occasionally slip into being less coachable. It happens, despite our best intentions, experience, and expertise. Perhaps it's when we are tired, hungry, not feeling well. Perhaps we have a real problem with the person giving us feedback. Whatever the issue, being coachable requires constant self-awareness and effort.

Coaching Up - When the Team Needs to Coach the Boss

As I began working with some of the most senior leaders, I found it true that it is lonely at the top. These leaders often found themselves in situations where they could not confide in many people, sometimes having nobody with whom they could open up completely, and often did not receive open and honest feedback from their teams. Coaching "up" the organization is often harder than coaching "down" when supervisors or managers coach the people reporting to them. It's basically the same as when a high school or college sports team has concerns with a coach, but are afraid to share the concerns directly with the coach.

I recall when I was the new human resources business partner for the top leader of a global organization. This leader was a genius about the business and had a lot of power within the company, but he was having a bit of trouble with the morale of his top 20 or so global leaders. He was a tough leader at times, demanding high performance because he was deeply committed to driving the organization as hard as he could to make it as successful as possible. He set stretch goals"intended to push the members of his team beyond what they may have thought was possible. The manner in which he challenged his leaders would occasionally slip into sarcasm or dismissive. In doing this, he also developed a reputation for not wanting to hear negative feedback, especially about his style, the direction of the organization, or other decisions he had made. As I worked with this leadership team, I was picking up on some of these concerns from the team members. Some would avoid speaking directly with the boss. Others would complain to me or openly among the broader team. So I asked the senior leader if I could reach out for feedback from his entire top team on his leadership style and effectiveness. To me, he expressed a sincere desire to hear feedback from the team, but since I didn't really know him well yet, I wasn't sure. And I knew that at least some of his team was convinced that this leader did not really want to hear feedback — they were convinced that he was not coachable.

So I set out to gather observations and advice from the team on both what this leader was doing well and how this leader may improve from the perspective of his global team. Some readily gave me brutally honest thoughts, complaints, and advice immediately. Others were afraid that if they were "too honest," it may come back to bite them if the leader found out who said what. So I made personal phone calls and visits to each person to assure them that their input was important to this leader and that all comments would be managed with care, without sharing any names as to who said what. Then, armed with unfiltered comments, I summarized all input on both what the leader was doing well and where the team members didn't think he was doing so well. It was a full report of brutally honest feedback.

Before I submitted the summary to the senior leader, I remember pausing and wondering if he was truly ready to see the feedback. Was he coachable? Did I protect the identity of those with the most critical feedback? As I said, often the top leaders of a company become insulated from feedback. Because of their lofty positions, their record of success, their knowledge or skills, and the drive that got them to where they are, it is not uncommon for a senior leader to become deaf to feedback. Or worse, at times they don't really care. However, in this case, I submitted the summary, I waited a couple days, and just as I started to get nervous that this leader was not happy to see what his team had shared, he replied to me saying, "This is humbling and so helpful. Thank you!" I remember speaking with him after that and being thrilled to see how appreciative he truly was, even though some of the feedback was harsh and had to be difficult for him to read. With great satisfaction I watched his behaviors change in team meetings, in smaller group settings, and even in his broad communications with the entire global team. Certainly, he would make mistakes, some of the very same issues that his team identified. But when that happened, either he would catch it after the fact or I had the opportunity to more easily point them out and not let small issues or misunderstandings become a bigger problem by not being addressed. My role shifted from being a "go between" for the team and the leader to more of another set of eyes and ears that could pick up the comments, body language, and less subtle cues of how the team was working together and the leader's impact.

That leader kept working at becoming a better leader by being coachable, though never perfect, and proceeded to have an even more exceptional career.

Being Coachable in a Family

The home can often be the most difficult place to be coachable. How often do you get mad at your parents for telling you what you need to hear, even when you know they are right? But even when they are right, it can still be hard to hear, can't it? And it's even harder when the "advice" comes from a brother or sister — what the heck gives them the right to tell you what you should do, right? Don't we at times show more respect to our friends, our coaches, and our teachers than we do to our own parents or siblings? Don't we at times respond to what somebody else tells us we should do even though we have been hearing that same thing from our parents for quite some time and did not respond to the advice? But despite the natural tendency to get angry when you are getting advice, direction, or flat out being told exactly what you should do, if you are able to be coachable in your own family, to work through the tendency to get defensive or upset, and help establish a culture of being coachable in your family, you will help build a stronger family, be a role model for others to follow, and will continue to grow as an individual.

Couples Coaching Each Other

I mentioned that my wife, Sue, was a tremendous athlete, including captain of her highly successful collegiate basketball team and then later becoming a PGA golf professional. One of her attributes was being extremely coachable. She would listen to her coaches, observe other players, and would immediately incorporate improvements in her sports. However, as coachable as she was in athletics, it was a different ballgame when her husband (me) would have a "suggestion." And I have to admit, the same would happen to me. I would somehow be able to take even sarcastic criticism from my childhood buddies, but if that same criticism would come from my spouse, it wouldn't be taken with the same sense of humor. Family dynamics are filled with emotion, including deep love, which is both a benefit and a challenge when sharing suggestions intended to help each other. At times, we are so comfortable with our spouse/boyfriend/ girlfriend that we easily slip into being "raw" with our emotions and our words, and quite frankly just get mean with each other.

"Be nice!" We've probably heard that command since we were toddlers. Yet it will apply to your entire life with respect to coaching and being coached. Even when you must receive or give difficult feedback or sternly address a significant behavioral problem, remember that simple command, "be nice."

And as you get older and perhaps have a spouse of your own, your ability as a couple to share observations and suggestions with each other about your relationship, to listen to each other when one has a concern, to take advice in a healthy appreciative way, to "be nice" at all times with each other, and then act to address any concerns or suggestions, your relationship will have the foundation to grow into what you both desire. This is not only possible, it is a requirement for healthy close relationships.

And when you have children of your own, your ability as a couple to role-model "being coachable" will return back to you with children who themselves will grow to be coachable.

What Does "Being Coachable" Really Look Like?

When a coach, teammate, parent, boss, sibling, spouse or friend is sharing their observations or thoughts on your performance, behavior, or specific actions, consider the following:

- **Open-Up**: *Decide* to be open and *show* that you are open to their thoughts. This includes making good eye contact and having body language and facial expressions that encourage others to share their observations and impressions, showing that you are always open to seeing yourself through their eyes. You may even ask for some advice or suggestions to get even better, which is the most obvious sign of being open to coaching. This takes courage, so decide up front to be courageous.

- **Listen**: Truly listen to what they have to say. Fight the tendency to explain or debate, at least at first before you've had the chance to hear, understand, and think about it a bit. I laugh at the memory of when my Coach Buck would say, "Popp, I ain't interested in hearing you talk!" Those were the times to simply listen to the coach.

- *Ask (if you must)*: Only if you truly do not understand the feedback, ask for clarity. There is a risk of asking too quickly and asking too much — which can easily coming off as being defensive — so handle questions with care when you are receiving coaching or feedback.

- *Accept and Thank*: With your body language, eye contact, facial expression, and/or verbally, tell the giver of feedback that you understand and appreciate their effort to help make you better. Remember, it may have been difficult for them to give you the feedback. A simple "thanks" may be all you need to acknowledge and thank that person. If it's a coach, maybe a simple nod, thumbs up, or "got it, coach" will do the trick. Even if you disagree at that moment or may think that the feedback has an ulterior motive, just accept and thank then at this point. Again, be courageous, be strong enough to accept the feedback even when it might hurt, even when it might be unfair in the end.

- *Think & Decide*: Now give the feedback some thought. It might seem completely accurate, it might seem completely wrong and unfair, or anywhere in between. Try to objectively assess the feedback and decide what you might do about it to get better. This may even mean disregarding the feedback — *deciding to do nothing is a valid decision* if that decision is made objectively and after sincerely thinking about the feedback. So think about it and decide what to do with that feedback.

- *Act:* Get Better! If you decide it is appropriate to take action on the feedback, then *act immediately*. This may mean an immediate change in routine or behavior or to simply be more "on the look-out" for when a certain behavior or action pops up. You may decide to have a discussion with your coach, parent, teacher (the giver of the feedback) after you've had the chance to think about what was said. Don't put off getting better, take action immediately whenever possible. Ultimately, being coachable is owning the responsibility of self-improvement and taking the actions necessary to grow and get better. We'll expand on this in Lesson #3 (Play Your Position Well) and Lesson #6 (Bias for Action).

In a nutshell, *be open, listen, accept, thank, think, and act* on all feedback. Ask questions *only* if you are truly unclear about the feedback, but for the most part, be quiet, maintain good eye contact, say thanks, and then decide & act as you think is best to get even better. Be prudent throughout this process. You don't have to blindly accept coaching and be forced to change; you are empowered to make the best of the gift of feedback. Either way, whether you have implemented a change or not, you may even want to follow-up with the person who gave you feedback to share what you've done or simply to say thanks again — that is an excellent way to honor somebody else, show appreciation, close the loop on being coached, and building stronger relationships in the process.

Crucial Conversations

Another critically important aspect of being coachable is being able to have productive face-to-face discussions with a coach, teammate, teacher, boyfriend/girlfriend, spouse, child, etc. for a particular performance-related concern. Especially when the stakes are high and emotions are running strong, these are sometimes called "crucial conversations." Too often, especially for young people, but not only with young people, complaints are voiced *about* somebody but not *to* or *with* that somebody. *Speak directly with the person with whom you have a concern and/or from whom you want to hear feedback.* Doing this can be awkward and even gut-wrenching, but when appropriate, these conversations are critical and you must be able to effectively do this. Don't talk *about* your coach to others, talk *to* your coach. Don't complain *about* your friend, talk *to* your friend.

When you do this, ask for permission to have the crucial conversation. "Can I speak with you about my performance?" "Can I share with you some thoughts I have about how it's going on our team?" "Would it be OK for me to share a concern that I have?"

When you give feedback during one of these important discussions, make it direct and constructive. Avoid complaining without offering ideas on what might be a better approach, whether you are talking about your own performance or about a concern that you may have with the team or with your coach, boss, spouse, etc.

Many Eyes and Ears for Infinite Growth

When you are not coachable, you simply limit your own growth. You'll only improve to the degree that your one set of eyes can see, your one set of ears can hear, and your own ability to spot your own strengths and opportunities objectively exists or not. And you can trust me when I tell you that *only you see you as you see you*!

When you are coachable, you have the fundamental building block to constantly improve through the eyes and ears of as many people as you wish to tap into — formally and informally. When you are coachable, *it is never too late* to turn things around or to take your performance to the next level.

Being coachable opens yourself up to an endless source of opportunity to improve and makes your growth potential infinite.

Warren Buffett, one of the most successful businesspersons in history says this about a team that embraces being coachable from all directions, "Surround yourself with people that push you to do better. No drama or negativity. Just higher goals and higher motivation. Good times and positive energy. No jealously or hate. Simply bringing out the absolute best in each other."

Thought Leaders and Role Models on Being Coachable

Legendary Dallas Cowboy football coach, **Tom Landry**, once offered a helpful perspective on what a coach is, saying, *"A coach is someone who tells you what you don't want to hear, who has you see what you don't want to see, so you can be who you have always known you can be."*

"It's what you learn, after you know it all, that counts."

– John Wooden,
arguably the best college basketball coach in history

"Coaching isn't therapy. It's product development, with you as the product."

– Fast Company

Your Choice: Will you Be Coachable?

Lesson #2: Be a Great Teammate

L esson #2 is also super powerful. It is one of the most intuitive and obvious bits of advice, yet can be one of the most difficult to follow.

Vince Lombardi, the Hall of Fame NFL Football Coach of the World & Super Bowl Champion Green Bay Packers, and the namesake for the Super Bowl trophy (The Lombardi Trophy) put it this way, *"Individual commitment to a group effort-- that is what makes a team work, a company work, a society work, a civilization work."*

Great Teammate in the Athletics

Of course teamwork is critical in athletics. It's all about the team in sports, right? Not so fast. Before you give the obvious answer, really think about how you're viewing teamwork.

Right now, is your focus and worry *more* on your own playing time or statistics than the success of your team? Is your focus *more* on being all-conference yourself than on your team being a conference champion? Are you *more* passionate about being a state champion than being named all-state? Do you lift your teammates up as a positive force or rely on them to bring you up?

If you cannot honestly answer these questions by picking your team above your own personal accolades, please listen up.

You're on a team. It is now less about you and more about the team.

Being a part of a good team is one of the most gratifying experiences one can have, even if the team does not experience a lot of wins. But when a team does in fact succeed, the feeling is irreplaceable. Picture the locker room after a Super Bowl championship, World Series, State Championship, or simply beating your #1 rival. Hugs, smiles, tears, dumping various drinks over each other's heads - celebrating together. There is nothing like it outside of sports.

Certainly, there are times to lead as an individual and times to follow, times to pick up your teammates and even times to get in their faces if they are not performing for the team. But the clear priority must be the performance of the team.

Accountability in sports is *not letting your teammates down because you don't want to let your teammates down,* not because somebody else is "holding you accountable."

Luisburg College National Champions

My son Sam was blessed to have a fantastic team experience in his first year of college when his soccer team, the Luisburg College Hurricanes from Luisburg, North Carolina, won the National Junior College Athletic Association (NJCAA) Division I men's soccer national championship, beating Tyler Junior College from Tyler, Texas, in double overtime. When I asked Sam what made that team so special, he talked about his teammates. One by one, he explained how each individual was so different from each other (i.e. from different countries and states, personalities, styles, sizes, interests, sense of humor, etc.) but that each brought their skills and leadership to the team and their focus was always on the team and each other. As Sam told me, for example:

> Max, from London, England, the best player on the team and the national player of the year, was humble, worked his butt off, and was simply a "good dude." Every player wanted Max's approval.

> Alex, from Paris, France, a second-year captain, worked hard on an off the field. From day one, he kept telling the team that we were special "as a team" and that we had what it took to win the national championship.

> Stevie, also from London, England, and another second-year captain, cared so much about the team. He played hard. And he would not hesitate to get in anybody's face if they weren't giving 100% to the team. "You're better than that!" was one of his classic lines as a leader.

> Robert, from Carey, North Carolina, didn't always start, wasn't flashy, and didn't get much recognition, but when he got his chances to play, he consistently played well and with passion. He covered for even the most recognized players on the team, whether he was given credit for it or not.

And just listening to Sam speak with admiration for his teammates and his desire to do whatever he could to help his team win a national championship, made it clear that he too was "all in" for that team. He transitioned fully from being an individual player to being a great teammate.

Sam went on further to explain how this team was different than any other he had been a part of when it came to playing as a team. But that didn't mean that they were always nice to each other. He told me how intense and competitive their practices would get. They would challenge each other physically and mentally, individually and in groups, yelling at each other, inter-squad trash talking, aggressively taking each other physically, head to head, body to body, and even the occasional attempt to cheat to get an intra-squad victory. As a team, the Luisburg Hurricanes of 2015 would not accept that they should lose any game, and that began in practice. Off the field, they had many different personalities and interests. On the field, their individual differences were put aside if it didn't help the team. Great teammates are able to compete extremely hard against each other in practice and leave it on the field when practice is over. And although they could come close to blows in practice, and there was the occasional apology for perhaps pushing the competition too far in practice, the team was united after the inter-squad competition, and especially united during games against other opponents.

I asked Sam why this was, why did the Luisburg team act like this, as great teammates even before the victories began tallying up, when other teams he has played for didn't quite get it like this even though those other teams were also winning most of the time. He said that the *goal was clear* to everybody, *to win the national championship*, and the goal was most important and above all other personal goals, interests, issues, or differences. He also said that the second-year guys (in their final season at the two-year junior college) showed confidence that the *goal was attainable (even expected)*, as those team leaders got close to the finals the year before but fell short of the championship. Finally, he said that the older guys also made it clear that even though the prior year's team had better talent, this team was a better team; this team had guys that put the *team above themselves. Those team leaders were more excited to have great teammates than to have better talent, and they expressed that fact openly to the new guys on the team. It became then a self-fulfilling prophecy.*

And forever I'll remember the scene, at the finals, seeing the winning goal in double overtime of the championship game slide past the goalkeeper and seeing the explosion of emotions from the players, coaches, trainers, and fans. The hugs, smiles, and tears of joy especially among those players will forever be etched in my memory. There is nothing like a team celebration immediately following a hard fought double-overtime championship.

To win any championship takes talent and a bit of luck at crucial moments, but I don't know of many, if any, sports teams that have won championships without great teammates, those who put the team above themselves.

A Star is Torn

A good friend and former teammate of mine, Brad, was a star running back in high school, highly recognized, and led his team to the state finals during his senior year. But when he arrived as a freshman to play college football, he was told that he was not going to be a running back anymore, but would instead be a linebacker. He was devastated at hearing this news and was thinking about quitting. To make matters worse, one of the other freshmen who would in fact continue to play running back was one of Brad's high school rivals from another school and who lived just down the road from Brad back in his home town. But instead of quitting, instead of pouting about not being a running back anymore, Brad decided to do what the coaches and the team needed from him. In the end, after four years, not only did Brad become a great linebacker, but he also developed into an outstanding special teams player and was ultimately voted Most Valuable Player by his teammates his senior year. And the other guy, Steve, Brad's former rival, who continued to play running back instead of Brad, ended up breaking every rushing record for Northern Michigan University and later played for the Green Bay Packers and the Pittsburgh Steelers in the National Football League. Both were great teammates and did what was best for the team. More important than their individual success, however, was that their teams during that time became among the best in NCAA division II football and, equally important, the two built a strong friendship along the journey.

Drafting for Great Teammates

Recently, I was listening to an annual conference "Arise with the Guys" that you can find at www.arisewiththeguys.com. One of the leaders and key speakers at this conference annually is former college and NFL football star and NFL football coach, Tony Dungy. Coach Dungy reiterated a point he has made on several occasions in saying the he always drafted players for character. His view is that talent alone is not going to win championships but wanted people of character and great teammates. Coach Dungy also wrote a book called *Uncommon* where he shares the importance of putting your own interests behind the interests of everybody else. He knows that is uncommon, not natural, but also emphasized that is what being a great teammate is all about. It is difficult to be uncommon, but it will bring you to a higher level of success and fulfillment in your life.

Great Teammate in the Workplace & Career

You'll rarely see the celebrations in the workplace as you'll see in athletics, probably never, but the same teamwork mindset as we just laid out in sports applies to the workplace. Challenge yourself to bring what you are learning today as a teammate with you into the workplace. And as I asked in the section above, challenge yourself with similar questions:

Will your personal career success be more important than the success of your team in the job you've chosen? Are you competing with your teammates in a way that diminishes their contribution or are you focused on being the best you can be for the team? Do you lift up your work partners as a positive force or wait for them to lift you up?

Employers want employees who are great teammates. Athletes have already learned how to be great teammates, even if it was learned by making mistakes. Just as in athletics, you're on a team when you enter the workforce. It must be less about you and more about the team.

Accountability in the workplace is: *not letting your work teammate down because you don't want to let your teammates and company down...* not because your management is "holding you accountable."

Although it is true that we all have very personal reasons for being at work — to provide for our family, to develop skills, to further our careers, to personally make a difference in the world, to be recognized as a success, to make money to buy things, and many other valid personal reasons to work where we decide to work — but when a team of people in a workplace recognize that their collective success is THE TOP priority and they pull together to achieve that team success, then the momentum of the successful team pulls the best out of every individual on the team, which in turn enables each individual on the team to achieve their own personal goals - an upward virtuous cycle.

The opposite is true as well. As a group of individuals struggles as a unit, then the downward momentum of the team drags the individuals downward also. As I observed and worked with several dysfunctional teams in the workplace, a common characteristic was that individual success or individual complaints trumped the care for teammates and for the success of the team. For a few examples, a leader that focused on their reputation more than the success of the team, team members being more focused on the faults of the leader or another teammate than the work and success of the team, or non-work related issues overshadow the mission of the team, too often held teams back, which in turn hurt every team member - a downward spiral that was almost impossible to stop without significant changes in the team members and/or the leader.

Ideal Team Player

One of today's best business management experts is author, speaker, and consultant Patrick Lencioni. He has worked with teams for about 25 years, has written multiple books, and is simply a good man. I became a big fan of Patrick several years ago through one of his most recognized books, *The 5 Dysfunctions of a Team*. More recently, he wrote another book called *The Ideal Team Player,* where he defines three virtues that make the ideal team player in his view based on his extensive work with teams:

Humble: He calls humility the antidote to pride — which he calls the root of all sin.

Hungry: Wanting to accomplish goals bad enough to work hard for it.

Smart: And by smart, he is not talking about ACT, SAT, GPA, or other individual-based academic accomplishment, though brainpower matters, but he is talking even more about emotional intelligence, caring for others and having the ability to personally and emotionally connect with and influence others in a healthy and productive way.[2]

These struck me as being as succinct and powerful a list as you can get, based on my experience with developing people and teams. You need all three, as Patrick makes perfectly clear.

---

[2] TEDx University of Nevada

Teammates can't only have one or two of these virtues to be "ideal" but must have all three. And as I am doing in this book, Patrick challenges his readers to assess themselves against these virtues and determine where they stand in each virtue, then work to close any gaps they may have. Again, this is the essence of being a great teammate and I'm happy to recommend Patrick as a wonderful resource for more learning in this regard.

Friend at Work

Gallup, Inc., is an analytics and advisory company that manages a popular and respected Employee Engagement Survey to assess employee engagement across many different types of companies. In their research, Gallup found that if an employee has a "best friend" at their place of work, then they tend to be more engaged in their work. Those that say they have a best friend at work tend to feel a higher level of trust, belonging, and inclusion at their place of work. Higher engagement means that person will generally give more effort in their job. Gallup finds that as more employees say they have a best friend at work, the companies sees improvements in areas such as less safety problems, higher customer engagement, and higher profits. In other words, with higher employee engagement, companies commonly see better business results. And having a best friend at work is one of the drivers of employee engagement.

I'll have to admit, having a best friend at work gets a little complicated at times and there are critics of Gallup for using this question. The critics argue that the question is confusing (Are you really talking about a best friend? Working directly with me? Isn't 'close' friend better?), is too narrowly worded ("best" means absolute top), is not statistically related to retention of talent, and other concerns. Also, there are some unintended issues and risks of being so close in the workplace — such as favoritism (perceived or real), teaming up against others in the office, spending too much time on personal matters, and the like.

Personally, I never had the level of friendship in my work career that would compare with the friendships I continue to have with my "old" friends from childhood and college, or the friendship I have with my wife and family — understandably.

However, I worked with many people who in fact truly had their best friends working with them and I saw the value of that close connection on a daily basis - caring for each other, clearly communicating, checking in when one seems down, taking a much-needed break or going out of the office for lunch, sharing a few good laughs, going out for dinner after work, and so on — all of the behaviors you should do as a good teammate whether you were best friends or not. I have in fact been on a few very special teams in my work career where that same type of care for a good friend existed across the entire team.

With that in mind, I can easily draw a comparison between "best/good/close friend" and "great teammate." Doesn't your good friend put your friendship above their individual interests? Will that close friend jump to your aid when you need it, almost regardless of what they are doing? And wouldn't you do the same for a good friend?

To me, it is clear that the concept of "close/good/best friend" in the workplace and "great teammate" are referencing the same base characteristics and, once achieved, results in the same fruits for the team — team and business results with more joy along the journey of achieving those results.

Teamwork in Large Companies

I recently had a conversation with a colleague of mine, Mary, who is an expert in organization development. We worked together for many years at Ford. Mary had also worked at GE, back in its heyday, prior to working at Ford. She has had many firsthand experiences with some of the best business organizations, teams, and leaders in the world and has also seen and worked with many dysfunctional teams as well. We were discussing our observations as to where GE may have lost its way recently, after being the model for organization effectiveness for so many years in the past. We also talked about our time at Ford when we worked with organizations that were "hitting on all cylinders" (that's automotive talk for doing well) and we also talked about examples of other organizations that were struggling to perform. For those struggling organizations, Mary recalled one experience when the senior-most leader of a global operation was trying to bring the team closer together, at a time when the company needed this critical organization more than any other team in world. At that time, Mary recalled the leaders of the various regions, as she put it, "...all were running their own show. [Saying] 'We're good. We don't need to come together as a leadership team.' " She recalled the difficulty in getting these leaders to view the overall team as their *first team*; they didn't want to give up any power for their own unit within the larger team. But this happens all the time. Leaders who are more concerned about themselves and their own piece of the larger puzzle are simply not team players. They might believe they are team players with their respective business unit teams, but fail to embrace the larger team as their priority, their first team. When this happens, the larger organization, the most important team, suffers; which then eventually hurts the smaller units within the larger organization - again, the downward spiral of bad teams.

Teamwork Drives Success (Alan Mulally)

Speaking of Ford, I must acknowledge one of the best leaders with whom I've had the pleasure to work with on a few occasions, and arguably one of the most successful leaders in business history — Alan Mulally. Alan spent most of his career with The Boeing Company making airplanes and then joined the Ford Motor Company as CEO in 2006. Many articles and books were written about the incredible turnaround that Alan led while at Ford. Under Alan's leadership and partnership with Chairman of the Board Bill Ford, Jr., another icon in business, Ford went from losing about $14 billion in one year alone, almost going bankrupt, with an anemic financial balance sheet, terrible stock performance, weak product lineup, and several other troubling business conditions, and turned it into a company that weathered a global recession, avoided bankruptcy, did not accept government bailout money, and went on to consistently make billions of dollars in profits consistently for several years.

But the most important part of Alan's strategy was that he led the transformation of the company to become one team, working on one plan, with one goal. A critical component of Alan's approach to the business was his approach to people and the culture. One of the four core elements to the 'One Ford Plan' was "working together as one global team." Forever I will recall fondly Ford's mantra, "One Team, One Plan, One Goal." The plan included One Ford Leadership Behaviors, a clearly defined list of a dozen behaviors expected of every team member. And if a team member could not live up to the expected behaviors, regardless of how smart, talented, or experienced they were, Alan would not hesitate to address that person, even if it meant making a change on the team. This was always done with respect and as honorably as possible, but it was clear that those who could not put the team above their individual interests or their piece of the larger organization would not be a part of this team. It was a powerful message to everybody when very senior leaders were added or removed from the top team based on being a great teammate, or not.

Wendy's CEO - Team Over All-Stars

Todd Penegor, my friend and former high school basketball and football teammate from Iron Mountain, Michigan, is now the CEO of Wendy's, the highly successful international fast food restaurant chain. Todd was a great teammate as a young athlete which helped form his philosophy as a prominent corporate leader today, similar to that described above. Todd said it this way to his global leadership team in a personal message:

"A focus on the team rather than individuals is an important part of my leadership approach as well. I want a championship team that works very well together, not a collection of individual all-stars. I focus on creating teams that always have each other's backs and want to win as a team. When we do that, great things happen for everyone. With this approach, I have continually seen people grow into bigger opportunities at Wendy's. Sometimes they have an opportunity for bigger roles elsewhere. We hate to lose anybody, but we are always proud to have great alumni growing across many organizations. The one thing I try not to tolerate for too long are people who believe it is all about them…even if they are talented. It can't be only about "what" you do…the "how" you do it is equally as important."

Although I miss the days when Todd snapped me the football and when I would feed him the basketball, I especially miss every game-day when his mother would make me chocolate chip cookies with m&m's for good luck. Maybe that's why I remember him as a great teammate!

Great Teammate in the Family

And yet again, the same mindset and advice to be a "great teammate" applies to a marriage and family. When you're in a marriage and family, it is less about you and more about your marriage and your family.

Will your personal success in your career, hobby, or personal wellness be more important than the success and wellness of your marriage and family? Do you lift your family up as a positive force to be stronger?

Accountability in a marriage and family is *not letting your spouse and kids down because you don't want to let your spouse and kids down*, not because your spouse or kids are "holding you accountable."

Family Decisions

I've mentioned that my wife was a great athlete and obviously I see her as a great person or I wouldn't love her as much as I do. I also mentioned in Lesson #1 that we took some time early in our relationship to settle into being coachable with each other. The same thing happened to us in becoming a great team as a couple, as parents. We are quite typical among many married couples in that we both came out of school with aspirations of having successful work careers, following our rewarding athletics experiences. I began in human resources and Sue began in finance, first in banking and then in office administration for a dental practice. Sue later switched careers and became a PGA golf professional. As a team, we were quite content with how our lives operated as we pursued our own professional and personal goals while building a stronger marriage.

Then, we began having children, which shifted our goals and challenged us to think about how best to work as a team to be good parents as our new top priority, while still delivering on our other career and personal objectives. We needed to become even better teammates, to focus on the success of the team (the family) beyond the success of any one individual. After working through several options, we agreed it was best for Sue to focus on giving golf lessons rather than working at a country club 6 days per week during the golf season as she had been doing. This change provided the flexibility that we both wanted to best support our young children while enabling both of us to continue with our careers. My choices for work assignments were now influenced primarily by the needs of our family, which at times were not what would have been best for my career. Fortunately, Sue's new flexibility became flexibility for our family overall. A few years later, we were able as a family to accept a job offer that took us to Mexico City for almost four years. This move turned into one of the most important and incredible growth journeys for us as a family, for each of us personally, and for my professional development and career opportunities.

Following that assignment in Mexico City, I was offered a big promotion that would have taken us to Sao Paulo, Brazil, which I was ready to accept on the spot. But I knew that this decision was a family decision and took it to my favorite teammate, Sue, and to our young sons. After discussing the options, we decided not to take the opportunity in Brazil in order to move back closer to our broader family in the U.S.

My point of sharing this story is not to say that our decisions were right or wrong, but it is to highlight that through our teamwork, Sue and I have been able to adjust personal careers, where we lived, and how we functioned as a family to enable us to deliver first for our family priorities (the team), and with those decisions, we have been able to thoroughly enjoy the journey along the way. I clearly benefited professionally with our agreed career decisions as Sue took on the majority of the work at our home. With that added support, my career success generated even better financial benefits for our family.

Fortunately, Sue enjoyed her work even more than I did. She decided not to go back to teaching golf, and instead became active in our church, our sons schools, gardening, and coached youth basketball, to name a bit of her new career portfolio. Some of her friends questioned why Sue would pause or change her professional career, but that was, for her, the obvious career and life choice at that time, and was the best for us as a family. Sue has never needed others to validate her career or family choices or to define her success - a tremendous character strength for her. We both found passion in our work, were able to provide financially, and the added flexibility enabled us to keep our family as our top priority as a team.

Again, my point here is not to say what working or family care arrangement is right or wrong, but to highlight what great teammates look like in families. This happened to work well for us. As you face your own career choices as a family team, you may make different decisions and choices. There is no right or wrong, except for what is right or wrong for you and your family at the time of your choices.

Finally, as our sons became old enough to weigh into our family decisions, we included them more and more prominently, to the point that we lean on them for advice now. They learned at a young age to think "family first." This journey was not always easy and we had our moments of overload, doubt, selfishness, and insecurity. But it has worked because we have become great teammates.

Without a doubt, being a great teammate in the family ensures and strengthens the most important lifelong meaningful bonds a person will ever have.

Teamwork in Society and Communities (COVID-19)

Before I close this lesson, I feel compelled to use the high point (or low point depending how you look at it) of the COVID-19 Pandemic experience as a fertile ground to highlight how important teamwork is in society and in our communities and a way to check ourselves with a real life example outside of athletics.

Did you place the team (your community) above yourself during the pandemic? Did you practice safe procedures, informed by the health experts and based on your own sound judgement?

Did you hold yourself accountable to help the bigger team, even if it meant for you as an individual to experience inconvenience or more difficult hardships?

Did you help calm the anxiety of those who tended to panic or did you make it worse? With all of the political rhetoric and hatred being thrown around, especially by certain media outlets and in social media, did you pile on with more hatred and negativity, or did you rise above and encourage messages of unity and solutions?

Did you reach out to help in ways that you knew you could help without adding unnecessary risk to yourself or to others?

And based on being a great teammate, did you find a certain level of joy in knowing that you were doing the right thing for the team, despite the actions that may not have been what you wanted personally?

On one hand, the world's reaction to the COVID-19 Pandemic was a once-in-a-lifetime display of teamwork with hundreds of millions of people doing their part to battle a common invisible enemy, virtually controlling its spread and getting through some of the most difficult times of our lifetime.

On the other hand, the crisis also highlighted many individuals (poor teammates) who put their own interests ahead of the best interests of the team. Most disappointing to me were those who continuously put political agendas ahead of resolving the issues in front of them, those who spread more fear and hate rather than helping quash anxiety and negative emotions, media outlets who simply leveraged the crisis to bash their targeted rivals and support their agenda, and those who decided that their personal convenience and priorities were above that of society or their local communities.

I hope you can look at your COVID-19 pandemic experience and be proud of being a great teammate. And if not, then think about how you can make changes right now to in fact make a bigger contribution.

Smile and Laugh More

Smile and laugh more.*

* note: this is the shortest paragraph in this book. So read it again a couple times!

Thought Leaders and Role Models for Being A Great Teammate

Legendary college and olympic basketball coach **Mike Krzyzewski** adds to this topic with, *"To me, teamwork is the beauty of our sport, where you have five acting as one. You become selfless."*

"People who work together will win, whether it be against complex football defenses, or the problems of modern society."

— Vince Lombardi,
NFL Hall of Fame coach of the Green Bay Packers and namesake of the Super Bowl trophy

It is fitting to consider what the founder of the Ford Motor Company, **Henry Ford**, said about teamwork, *"Coming together is a beginning. Keeping together is progress. Working together is success."*

"Trust is knowing that when a team member does push you, they're doing it because they care about the team."

– Patrick Lencioni,
author and management guru

Harry S Truman, 33rd President of the United States and leader of the U.S. through the victory of World War II, the fight against communism, and the post-war rebuilding

Europe, said this about teamwork, *"It is amazing what you can accomplish if you do not care who gets the credit."*

Final Thought on Being a Great Teammate

In closing Lesson #2 - Be a Great Teammate, I hope it is clear to you that regardless of the sport, workplace, family, or even in the broader community and society at large, the fruits of being a great teammate include lifelong meaningful bonds way beyond the sport or the job, professional success and fulfillment, stronger marriages and families, and more successful communities.

Almost all of the best friends in my entire life were my teammates as a younger person. It could be the greatest gift that athletics can bring to a young person and can last a lifetime. Don't let that opportunity pass you by.

Your Choice: Will you be a Great Teammate?

Lesson #3: Play Your Position(s) Well

This next lesson could have easily been a part of Lesson #2 - Be a Great Teammate because a critical aspect of being a great teammate is playing your position well. However, because there are several other important aspects of playing your position well, I wanted to highlighted this one its own.

In Lesson #2 - Be a Great Teammate, we focused primarily on the selfless nature of being a great teammate. I asked questions about whether the team was more important to you than your own personal accomplishments. I wanted that to be the most important aspect of Lesson #2. So now, assuming you buy into the concept of team as the highest level of importance, let's shift our focus onto the critical importance of you playing your part, playing your position to the best of your ability, for both yourself and for the team.

You Play Several Positions

The reality of life is that you play several "positions" at any one time covering all aspects of your existence. This lesson is focused on the most important roles, positions, or jobs that you have at any one time. And those roles change with time. With that in mind, it is important to first be completely self-aware and recognize all of the roles you play, the positions you have, and the jobs you are performing and are expected to be performing.

These positions or jobs may include roles such as:

- Student studying computer science
- Center on the basketball team
- Special Teams expert in football
- Waiter at the local restaurant
- Big sister to two brothers
- Child living & helping at home
- Roommate with a group of peers
- Worker on a landscaping crew
- Volunteer at church
- Etc.

For those critical positions that you have chosen to play — and perhaps one or two for which you were "volun-told" without much of a choice — the heart of this lesson is to *play those positions to the best of your ability.*

Your Team is Counting on You to Play Your Position Well

For every position you play, you most likely have a team connected to that position and your team is counting on you to be excellent in playing that position. There cannot be any other position even close to as important to you than the position you play; nobody has more influence over that position than you do and nobody else has the accountability that you have to play that position. You must own each of your positions and step up to perform each with excellence.

To play your position well, begin with being honest about your strengths and weaknesses, your work ethic, your commitment, and your attitude. Constantly work on improving on these core characteristics. Avoid focusing on the things that somebody else needs to do to get better, whether that is your coach, teammates, boss, girlfriend/boyfriend, parents, referees, political leaders, media personalities,....the list can be endless. You focus on you when it comes to your own performance. Again, your team is counting on you to play your position well.

Check Yourself

When you look in the mirror, can you look the person staring back from the glass in the eye with respect to giving all you can to play your positions well? Are you doing all you can to be the best version of yourself in each of the positions you play? Are you being equally effective in both *what* you do and *how* you do it? And as you play your positions, are you still focused on the success of the broader team? Do you bring positive energy to your team?

Playing Your Positions Well in the Athletics

Every position matters in athletics. In football, if you're a lineman, for example, then you must sign up to getting bigger and stronger, getting quicker feet, knowing your assignments, knowing how to make your calls at the line. If you're a kicker, you are expected to kick thousands of balls, establish your pre-kick routine to help master the mental aspect of kicking under pressure, and do all you can to be able to deliver the big field goal when the clock shows only a few seconds left and your team is down by one or two. Goaltenders need to master the crease.

With every sport and every position, you are expected to play your position well so that the team has the best chance to win. Your team is relying on you to do your job. Don't let the team down. Deliver your job for the success of the team.

Your coaches aren't and won't be perfect. Fact.

Your teachers aren't and won't be perfect. Fact.

Your teammates aren't and won't be perfect. Fact.

The referees aren't and won't be perfect. Fact.

And guess what, you aren't and won't be perfect. However, although you have zero control and very little influence over the others listed above, you have virtually total control over yourself. So focus on what you must do to play your positions well. Too many athletes, especially younger players, focus an extraordinary amount of time on the imperfections of their coaches, teammates, parents, and referees, and too little on their own opportunities to improve. Even when there is valid reason to complain about a coach, teammate, parent, or official, it simply isn't worth the energy or the distraction from your own preparation and performance.

Coaches coach, teachers teach, parents parent, refs ref, and players play — you focus on playing your position to the best of your ability and stay away from coaching, parenting, or playing somebody else's position.

But Recover the Fumble!

It is important to mention in this lesson that although your focus must be on playing your position and doing your job, you must also keep your eyes and ears open to jump in as needed to help the team when you are able to and needed to help the team. For a clear analogy, the entire football team may be executing their individual jobs perfectly during a play, but if that ball is fumbled, every single person must dive for the fumble and fight like a hungry dog to recover it until the officials pull them off of the pile. Although your clear top priority is to do your job well, never let your focus on your job make you blind to a critical need of the team. There is an important balance between Lesson #2 - Be a Great Teammate and Lesson #3 - Play Your Position Well. The team is still the priority and the team is relying on you to play your position well. This principle will also play out in the workplace and in your family later in this lesson. So play your position well, but always be ready to dive on the fumble!

Give Yourself Credit When Credit is Due

When you evaluate your own performance, objectively assessing in how you played or are playing your position(s), don't be afraid to congratulate yourself for achieving what you've set out to achieve. This isn't meant to be boastful or public, but instead a private subtle way to give yourself a figurative pat on the back. Or, consider this one. I recall my former college football teammate, Chuck, who, following college, played with great success both in the Canadian Football League and then as a Miami Dolphin in the NFL.

Chuck was a confident young man and not afraid to assess his own accomplishments, good or bad. I remember vividly following our last home game of the season when Chuck's roommates noticed a huge cake in the refrigerator that had "Congratulations Chuck" written in frosting across the entire cake, which filled a complete rack in the fridge. When the roommates asked Chuck who bought him the cake, he replied, "I did. I had a great year!" So funny. Your self-pat-on-the-back may not go that far, but you've got to love Chuck's ability to recognize himself for playing his position well.

Parents Playing Their Position - Stay in Your Lane

One of the biggest challenges for my wife and me as parents of young athletes, especially after both being athletes and youth coaches for many years, was to play the position of parents, to "stay in our own lane" as parents. Like most parents, we watched our own kids struggling with learning their sport, having issues with their coaches or teammates, and witnessed what looked to us like inadequacies and unfairness on one of their sports teams. In other words, we watched what was normal in youth sports. But is was difficult for us not to want to insert ourselves as parents on behalf of our children — it was especially difficult for me. I caught myself on occasion projecting my own athletic and professional experience and expectations onto a youth sports program or coach and then was itching to get involved to "fix" it. In a few unique cases, getting involved was appropriate. However, in 99% of the cases in my experience, the best thing to do was to simply love our children — to let coaches coach, to support the team and program, to avoid openly complaining about coaches, organizers, or other players, to avoid criticizing officials, and instead simply be a great fan of the sport and support the team on which our child was participating. That's playing the position of the parent well. Easy right? Oh I wish it were so.

I've certainly had a few regretful moments in my life when I "stepped out of my lane" to complain about or challenge a coach, referee, another parent, or a player on the team, either directly to them or complaining to other people about them. As a young athlete, I recall getting a few technical fouls (aka Tee'd Up) in basketball for my hot headed reaction to a referee's call. As a parent, I can recall distinctly a couple incidents where my emotion got the better of my intelligence. And that moment immediately after weakness prevails and you step out of your lane are as embarrassing as they come — especially when your own child, parent, or close friend sees it. To make it worse, in a split second, you know you can't get that moment or that behavior back once you let it out. These mistakes will last in your memory for a long time, perhaps forever, which is probably a good thing if it prevents it from happening again.

I read a great sign at a youth hockey arena that gives parents something valuable to keep in mind. The sign said:

"Your child's success or lack of success in sports does not indicate what kind of parent you are. But having an athlete that is coachable, respectful, a great teammate, mentally tough, resilient, and tries their best IS a direct reflection of your parenting."

Doing Your Job Well - Workplace and Career

There is nobility in having a job and working hard in that job, regardless of the level of income, the fame and notoriety that job may or may not bring, or the level of recognition one may receive for doing a job. If you are fortunate enough to have a job, whether it pays or not, but especially if it pays you for your work, you have a job to do, no matter how you got there, and you are expected to do that job. With any job, you have a decision to make every day to either return to that job or not. And when you decide to go to that job on any particular day, you are also deciding to do that job to the best of your ability. At least that's this part of Lesson 3: Do your job well.

Over the long haul, it will be more satisfying to you to do a job for which you have passion, for which you apply your skills and abilities, and through which you contribute to a worthwhile cause. Your satisfaction in doing that job well will be more important than the amount of money you make, the notoriety you get, or the status it gives you. This may not sound exactly right to you especially in today's culture with so much focus on wealth, fame, and material possessions. Certainly, making a lot of money for doing a job is not a bad thing at all, is desired by most people, and it is in fact possible. But as a person who has studied and worked in the "people business" for almost three decades, I firmly believe that, once a person's basic life necessities are covered financially, more important than the pay for a job is the satisfaction a person gets for using their skills to do good work and make an impact on a worthwhile cause. There are many who make a lot of money in a job and are not happy in that job and not happy with their lives. There is always more money to be made, more recognition to be garnered, and more material things to buy with more money. Any time I have come across a person who is clearly money-motivated well beyond other factors of job satisfactions, I have found that person struggling to enjoy their work and not a particularly good teammate. I have found those overly-focused on their personal earnings to allow that focus on money to detract them from focusing on their own development, on being a great teammate, and doing their own job extremely well.

Working for A Smile

A good friend of our family, Amy, is a professional interior designer and an actively involved mother of two impressive young men. Both Amy and her husband Bryan were talented athletes in their younger days and both have used athletics to grow personally, to help shape the character of their own sons, and to find mutual enjoyment as a family. I mention Amy in particular here because she is a wonderful example to me for selecting a job for which a person has passion to perform that job well. You see, Amy used to work in a job that may have seemed ideal to many in the interior design business; it had good pay, status, notable clients, and many of the other characteristics of what might be viewed as an excellent job. But for some reason, Amy decided to leave her seemingly ideal job, take a significant pay cut, and work for a non-profit business that serves individuals, families, and veterans who are coming out of homelessness. The company Amy works for now turns empty houses into homes for families most in need by using donated furniture and household goods and by using Amy's interior design talents to transform each house into a personalized, welcoming, and appropriately styled home. Often, the children in these families receive their own bed for the first time rather than sharing a mattress that sits on the floor. As Amy said to me, "I have had design clients with huge budgets and I have made a decent deal of money working on their projects and I thought that was fulfilling. But it wasn't until the work I do now that I realize that a child's smile seeing their bed off the floor is the most satisfaction I could ever hope to find in a job."

Losing Focus on Self, Here, Now

In my many years in corporate America, it was common for me to see and counsel people who weren't happy in their work. Studies over my career consistently showed the majority of people in the workplace were disengaged, unhappy, unfulfilled, or uninspired with their work, job, or career. But in my experience, through one-on-one career counseling sessions, focus group meetings, informal discussions, and general observations, the focus and worry of the majority of these unhappy folks was about *somebody else* not doing their job even more than they were sincerely critiquing their own performance, their own circumstances, and working to get better themselves.

Likewise, I saw and worked with many who were more worried about getting *their next job* rather than achieving excellence in performing their *existing job*. They would too frequently be asking for what they should be doing to get the job they wanted, asking if, for example, they network more with senior leaders, volunteer more for other projects outside of their current responsibilities, and asking about other considerations outside of their core job. To be clear, looking forward to your next job and taking action today to achieve that next job is definitely important to do, but when the search for the *next job* negatively impacts the performance on the existing job, everybody loses. The lack of focus on doing ones own job well now will hurt present performance and future career potential.

And just as I mentioned above in athletics regarding coaches, referees, parents, and teammates, your future bosses (supervisors, managers, directors, vice presidents, etc) and your future workmates won't be perfect either, just as you won't be perfect. You'll have some great bosses. I was blessed with several good ones, with a few being truly outstanding. You'll have some weaker bosses, as I did on occasion as well. You'll have some great workmates and perhaps in that same team you'll have some work partners that you will barely be able to work with on a daily basis. It just happens that way. But as you are learning now in athletics, if you can focus less on them and more on doing your job well for the success of the team, you'll perform better, you'll make the team more successful, and you will enjoy your work more.

I remember a few occasions when I personally allowed my focus to drift from doing my job well and focusing too much energy on my perception of my boss's inadequacies, or focusing too much on one particular workmate whose bad behavior I responded with my own bad behavior, or when I focused too much on issues that bothered me but were outside of my department and outside of my control and influence. And during those times, I remember my job satisfaction was at its lowest. Conversely, my job satisfaction and performance was at its best when my focus was primarily on doing my own job well, doing good work, and staying away from the noise that could distract me from doing my own job well, the noise that would keep me away from focusing on the value I was creating, the noise that would suck the energy and joy from my work.

Wendy's CEO Still Plays Lineman

Not only was Todd Penegor, the CEO of Wendy's, my high school teammate in basketball and football, but he was a great teammate and played his positions well as our top shooter in basketball and, in football, our center and leader of the offensive line. He also continues to be an excellent golfer. Athletics were a big part of his young life and that experience continues to shape how he looks at his job as CEO for the team at Wendy's. In a letter he sent to the entire global "Wendy's Family," Todd described his job as this:

> "For me, it starts with a servant leadership mentality. I believe it's my role to support all of you, your teams and the System. ...I try to be the big lineman that opens up the holes for my team to be successful. I want them to score the touchdowns and get the recognition for making the big plays that set us apart from the competition. I find satisfaction when I am able to put them in a position to do that. That's my job...to set the team up for success and to allow everyone to be their very best."

Although Todd was a recognized star in basketball and golf in his younger days, I love the fact that he has chosen to view his role as CEO as the guy with his hand in the dirt, the one who normally gets recognized only if called for a penalty, the one who creates the space for others to get into the end zone. There is something special about "linemen" — anybody who plays a position that is not easy, gets relatively little praise, involves dirt, bumps, and bruises, and is easily criticized for errors, but continues to get the job done despite all of that to make it possible for others to score.

Helping Put a Man on the Moon

There is a famous story from 1961 when President John F. Kennedy visited NASA for the first time. This was back at the time when the U.S.A. was attempting to put a man on the moon for the first time. During the visit, President Kennedy introduced himself to a man who was mopping the floor, the janitor, and the president asked the man what he did at NASA. The janitor replied, "I'm helping put a man on the moon!"

This janitor embraced his job as an important role of the overall mission of NASA and the U.S.A. at the time. He knew his part of that mission and was focused on doing his job well for the success of the entire team. And by doing so, he performed his job with the precision of his astronaut, scientist, and engineer teammates, and he was fulfilled in doing his job well.

Beautiful Retirement Party

Working in Human Resources for nearly 30 years provided me an opportunity to attend more retirement celebrations than I can remember. Especially in the early days of my career, some retirement parties were wedding-like, held at banquet halls with dinner, speakers, and presentations. Others were modest "get togethers" for a final toast and sendoff. Some were tearful subdued events while others were festive cheerful parties; and many were both. It didn't matter if the celebrations were for vice presidents, middle managers, or front line workers; each mirrored the character of the retiree after working for many years and, for some, even decades at the company. A few years ago, I attended the retirement party for my mother, who retired late into her 70's. She worked over 30 years in clerical roles for an electric company in my small hometown of Iron Mountain, Michigan. As my brother and I, along with our wives Sue and Laura, devoured our local favorite Italian raviolis during an informal retirement luncheon, we listened to the comments made by a few of the company's senior leaders, a couple of my mothers' co-workers, and the "line guys" who worked in the field on electrical power lines. I recall holding back tears of pride in how each described my mother's impact in the office and on this successful company. Though "only" a clerical worker (as some might call her), it was clear that by playing her positions well, whatever she was asked to do, along with her positive energy and attitude, was a driving force for the entire team. Through her three decades of working at this one company, she became the expert on how things operated in the office. She knew everybody's name and learned several different roles, which enabled her to fill in for others while they were on vacation and brought flexibility to the office when new work came their way. She enjoyed helping the team and even worried about retirement because "they need me," as she would say with joy. And her periodic cookies and other homemade treats were always appreciated by "the guys" in the office.

That retirement event and heartfelt comments were noticeably different from many of the retirement parties I had attended in my time, whether they were for highly recognized senior executives or team members lower in the organization. I remember the realization, after hearing those comments that day, then reflecting on how she lived her life, that my mother truly had a successful career. I've always known she was a fantastic mother, but that day shed her in a new light for me. What a beautiful retirement party it was for all of us. You would be blessed to be able to have that same experience one day.

Everyday Heroes

Somewhat similar to the NASA janitor or my mother, the Coronavirus pandemic highlighted everyday heroes that otherwise get little attention as being "successful" when compared with other professions, especially when compared with professional athletes, famous actors, media personalities, business leaders, and so on. Although doctors generally do get recognized as being successful in today's society, there were many doctors who went above and beyond the normal call of duty, shattering the image of not being flexible with their schedules or too accommodating to patients, putting themselves at risk of serious health issues and working incredibly long hours to help those with the virus and to help their teams manage through the fears and intense work for several weeks and even months. Add in all of the nurses doing the same. Think about all the good and noble public servants doing the same that they normally do, but in a more dangerous and emotionally charged environment. Then consider all of the grocery store workers, food service workers, volunteers at food banks, cleaners and janitors of all kinds, and many other professions that aren't usually looked upon as heroes or role models of professional success — but they were and are just that. Many of them can easily say that they have saved lives and are continuing to do so every day. Their pay will likely not change anytime soon; for some, perhaps a little pay increase, but others ended up losing their jobs due to the economic fallout of the pandemic. These everyday heroes may may get a fleeting moment or even a longer period of recognition or glory, though that will taper quickly in time. But these everyday heroes can rest assured that they've been successful in doing their jobs well, which saved lives and saved communities.

And let's never forget how this pandemic highlighted the importance of teachers in our communities. Many adjusted quickly to delivering classes remotely and/or enabling students and parents to homeschool. As parents found themselves becoming homeschooling teachers, many developed a newfound respect for what teachers do for their children every day during each school year. But what also became more clear to me and to many others is when teachers do in their jobs well, our children learn to love each other in the classroom, to love and be loved by a caring adult in the room. We often get laser focused on that AP class, GPA, ACT, or other measure of academic excellence, all of which have importance, but when that interaction with teachers and classmates are no longer there, "ah ha" that's what a good teacher brings in addition to the curriculum being taught.

Do the Right Thing

Doing your job well in the workplace also means *do the right thing at all times.*

One of the assignments I had for six years during my career was managing employee benefits for hundreds of thousands of employees, retirees, and their families. Unfortunately, this assignment occurred during the economic crisis of 2008 and for the years following. As my company was headed toward bankruptcy, as in fact happened to our closest competitors, we were forced to take drastic steps to stop the bleeding of cash from the company in order to avoid bankruptcy. It was a no-win situation. We cut spending everywhere possible, but tried to protect the core business. I recall the heart wrenching discussions we had as a leadership team on cutting back on certain employee benefits and job reductions. And we did in fact make benefit cuts and sadly reduced the salaried workforce by nearly 50% in the United States and in several other markets globally. As a result, my team and I personally received criticism from all angles. On one side, the company leadership needed to find even more ways to save money and so the pressure was continually on to save more money. On the other side, employees were desperate to save their own jobs and benefits. It was hard and thankless work. But in the end, we helped save the company without taking any taxpayer money from the government in the form of a bailout, we weathered the storm, and started rebuilding the company the right way. When we were able to bring back some of the reduced or postponed benefits, we did. When we could get back to providing pay increases, we did. Over the next several years, the company went on to fix the balance sheet, make better products, ensured competitive wages and benefits for employees, hired employees again, and worked together better as a team, all while consistently maintaining profitability. I look back at that time and can say that we did what we had to do for the team at that time we did the right thing — not for recognition, not because it was easy, not because it was popular, because it was none of these. We did the right thing for the future of the company and for our people.

To do your job well, you must believe in the company for which you're working, trusting that it will do the right thing. In my case, I was always proud to work for the Ford Motor Company. Sure, no company is perfect. But when you consider its history over 117 years and see how it stepped up in times of crisis — including making planes for World War II, being recognized consistently as a good corporate citizen, not accepting a government bailout during the Great Recession of 2008, pushing for and leading environmental innovations in manufacturing and energy, and stepping up early in the Coronavirus pandemic to halt vehicle production and make respirators and masks for medical professionals to combat the virus — I was able to work with confidence that in playing my positions well that I was helping a great company make positive impact for people and the broader society. And I can continue to have pride as a Ford retiree.

Recover the Fumble at Work Too!.... Play Special Teams When Needed

Way too often in the workplace, I have heard phrases like, "Not my job" or "That's above my pay grade" or "I don't get paid to do that" and other ridiculous comments that indicate poor teams and poor team players. These people are drawing rigid lines around what they do, thinking too much of self and not enough of the broader team or their customer, limiting their scope to only their specific job. These comments are like fumbles on the football field or loose balls on the basketball court. Dive on those situations and save the "ball", whether that is a customer needing to be directed somewhere else with care or if it's reaching out to another teammate who needs help. Be careful not to take this Lesson #3 - Doing Your Job Well too far into thinking that it overrides the importance of Lesson #2 - Be a Great Teammate. The team remains the priority, even when you are focused on doing your job to the best of your ability. So yes, you do get paid to help the team succeed first and to help your teammates if and when you are capable of doing so - it is your job to recover the fumble at work.

To further make this important point. Look at those who play special teams in the NFL, those who play on the kick-off team, kick-return, field goal unit, punt team, hands team, etc. These players don't get any more pay for doing this, they just do it. Steve Mariucci told me about a time when he was the head coach of the San Francisco 49ers and Hall of Fame receiver Jerry Rice put himself in on the kick-return team so that he could be sure that the kick-off was caught without any fumble! He only wanted what was best for his team in that situation.

Playing Your Positions Well in the Family

The most important position you'll ever play is that which you play in your family. And as you get older and have your own family, your positions in that family only get more and more important.

Help at Home

So what is your "position" or "job" in a family? Aren't families just families? I argue that you do in fact play a position, and probably multiple positions, within your family. You may have chores around the house (taking out garbage on garbage day, cleaning your room, raking leaves, cutting the grass, the list can be long), you may be needed to babysit your younger siblings, or help an older member of the family get to appointments, or many other responsibilities required to make your family function and to grow stronger. For some of this, you may even get an allowance, but when you stop and think about the effort you put into your chores, I'll bet you receive way more from your family than you can ever give by performing chores and duties around the house.

Family Reputation

Beyond any "work" that you do for your family, you also have a responsibility to uphold your family reputation, for representing your family to the best of your ability, by how you carry yourself, by how you treat others, by how you interact on social media, by your performance in school, sports, and other extra-curricular activities. This will always be an important part of your role, your position, your job.

Love Your Family

You also have the responsibility to love your family, your parents or guardians, your siblings, and extended family. This includes communicating with them as to what you are doing, what you are thinking, and asking them about the same. Allow them to be a big part of your life. In return, they will enhance your life. Your family will most often be the greatest source of happiness and fulfillment in your life.

At the same time, your family can be the most significant source of distress and frustration.

Your parents aren't and never will be perfect. Fact.

Your brothers or sisters aren't and never will be perfect. Fact.

Your future spouse won't be perfect. Fact.

Your future kids won't be perfect. Fact.

And again, as with athletics and in a job, you aren't and won't be perfect in playing your positions within your family. But this lesson is encouraging you to know the super-important position(s) you play in your family. Cultivate those critical relationships even when you feel overworked in school or stressed at a job; never let the family suffer for the other positions that you play.

Especially during high school, college, and early career when you are becoming more self-sufficient and quite capable, but you most likely still rely on your parents or other family members for important help — college search, tuition payments, vehicle expenses, spending money, food, clothing, place to live, etc. It is the phase where you are almost on your own, but not quite yet. You are the most capable of your life and needing less from your family than you've felt before, but you still need your family and they need you. Honor your parents and your broader family especially during these times. For you will never be more fulfilled than when you succeed with your family. And you will never feel so empty as when you fail your family. Play your family positions to the best of your ability.

Thought Leaders and Role Models on Playing Your Position Well

"There's no substitute for hard work. If you work hard and prepare yourself, you might get beat, but you'll never lose."

— **Nancy Lieberman** (nicknamed "Lady Magic")

former professional basketball player and coach in the Women's National Basketball Association (WNBA), NBA broadcaster, head coach of Power, and regarded as one of the greatest figures in American women's basketball.

"He is well paid that is well satisfied."

— **William Shakespeare,**
perhaps the most famous writer in history.

"Try not to be a person of success,
but rather try to become a person of value."

— **Albert Einstein,**
one of histories greatest scientists and thinkers.

"The greater danger for most of us lies not in setting our aim too high
and falling short; but in setting our aim too low and achieving our
mark."

— **Michelangelo,**
sculptor, painter and architect considered to be one of the
greatest artists of the Renaissance — and arguably of all time.

"There are two kinds of people, those who do the work and those who
take the credit. Try to be in the first group; there is less competition
there."

— **Indira Gandhi,**

Indian politician and a central figure of the Indian National
Congress. She was the first and, to date, the only female Prime
Minister of India.

Lesson #3 Summary

In summary, Lesson #3 - Play Your Position(s) Well is an encouragement to *own your job,* whether as a football player, volleyball player, laborer, professional, boyfriend/girlfriend, spouse, brother/sister, son/daughter, whatever are those top priority positions that you play. Ensure you are picking the right positions, the ones you know you should do and, whenever possible, the ones you have a talent and passion for doing. Once picked, own the responsibility of getting good at those positions, and then perform those jobs to the best of your ability. Play All of Your Positions Well.

Your Choice: Will you Play Your Positions Well?

Lesson #4: Master Adversity

The term "adversity" simply means difficulties, misfortune. Although this is a simple definition, adversity is everywhere and it shapes our lives. This is a major topic for life in general and one where athletics can and should be a fantastic training ground to prepare you for life's more serious challenges. Furthermore, "mastering" adversity goes beyond just getting through or surviving difficulties; mastering adversity means developing the ability to take control of your reaction to challenges and stepping up to be the *best version of yourself in the midst of your toughest times.*

When times are the toughest, when we are scared, hurt, sick, or worried, we learn things about ourselves that we may have never known. We hope that we will handle adversity well, but are never quite sure until actually faced with the real misfortune, the real pain, fear, and suffering. This lesson is about preparing for adversity, effectively dealing with adversity, and then learning from adversity, beginning with athletics.

Master Adversity in Athletics

"With adversity comes our greatest triumphs" Is the quote that opens a video trailer for one of the greatest stories in college sports. The Northern Michigan University Football Wildcats lost every single game of their entire season in 1974, despite being close in every one of those games, often leading into the 4th quarter of the game. The following season, in 1975, those Wildcats won the NCAA Division II National Championship, despite trailing in almost every game heading into the 4th quarter. That championship team did something no other team has done in the history of NCAA sports, not in any of the major professional sports, neither men's nor women's — to follow a winless season with a national championship.

The main difference? The difference was the way in which they prepared for and the way in which they handled adversity. According to one of members of that team, Jack Hirn:

> *"Simply put, (our coach) made it his mission for us to own the final quarter of the game," Hirn said. "We would raise four fingers at the start of the fourth quarter, which represented discipline, conditioning, motivation and effort. We trained and conditioned past the normal time of a game to create endurance in us. It drew out the toughness of many of the stronger guys, but also exposed those that didn't have it in them. Many were shown the door and had scholarships revoked. The players that endured this brutal spring training session would become the essential nucleus of the championship team."[3]*

In football, there will be fumbles, interceptions, losses, injuries, and bad calls by the officials. Basketball, baseball, and hockey will always have turnovers, errors, strikeouts, and the occasional blown calls by officials and umpires. Volleyball will have mis-hits, miscommunication, and blown calls by the

---

[3] Iron Mountain Daily News, April 2020

officials. And in all sports, fatigue, injury, self-doubt (choking), and mistakes will be a part of just about every game and every season, physically, mentally, and emotionally.

So how do you equip yourself for the ups and the downs of a game or season, the bad calls, injuries to yourself or to key teammates, all that you know will be part of the game and season?

First you must *recognize* the high probability, perhaps view it as a guarantee, that *you will run into these types of challenges*, especially the common challenges mentioned already. And then there may be other challenges that you would never expect - so you must also *expect the unexpected*. By recognizing the likelihood of these types of problems you are able to prepare yourself to handle both the highly likely (questionable calls by officials, fumbles, turnovers, bumps and bruises) and the unexpected.

A bit later in this book, in Lesson #5 - Peak Performance State, I will get into more detail on being mentally, physically, and emotionally prepared to be at your best, but for now suffice it to say that you must train for adversity and the unexpected. Before anything happens, you must think about how you'll handle injury, bad calls, bad weather, and also have a mindset that you will in fact successfully handle anything and everything that comes your way during practices, games, and the entire season. Physically, you must train for going beyond the normal limits of your sport, training for overtime, heat, cold, rain, noise, etc. And you must get to know yourself under stress — think about how you've handled stress and adversity in the past and learn from when you've handled it well and when you didn't handle it well. In other words, you must prepare yourself physically, mentally, and emotionally for problems that will most certainly emerge, as well as prepare more generally for challenges that you can't even imagine right now.

Then, when you find yourself in the middle of adversity, the most important first step is to *recognize the challenges you're facing and the emotions you're feeling.* What is most urgent? What needs attention now? What are you feeling? The urgent matters are usually pretty easy to see. But they aren't always the most important challenges or actions to take. Be aware that your emotions may begin to take over your rationale thinking - it's natural. So, to the degree possible, as the obvious challenges hit you in the face, force yourself to intentionally not let your emotions "hijack" your rational logical thinking. *Force yourself to keep the bigger picture in mind and make deliberate decisions to accomplish your main goal.* Be careful not to let the urgent matters that are in front of you and your natural emotions distract you from your greater purpose. You must tend to the urgent matters, but only when you've assessed that they fit the bigger picture and larger goal.

In athletics during a game situation, you may have just lost your best player to injury, or you may have just suffered a big hit or have just made a costly turnover, or you are playing a game in torrential downpour and the field is an absolute mess. Your natural emotions and thoughts of anger, fear, panic, etc. will undoubtedly emerge. However, if you have prepared in advance for the likelihood of adversity, recognize it, and take control of your thoughts and actions, you will be in the position to master adversity and not only survive it. Rather than lament the loss of your best receiver, you immediately focus on adjusting the plays to highlight your next biggest weapon. If the torrential downpour is making it too difficult to pass the ball, avoid getting angry about the wet muddy ball, bad throws, and dropped passes and shift to a creative running game.

Getting Cut and Getting Better

My son Isaiah was a skilled athlete from his earliest days in sports, from informal back-yard sports to playing highly competitive travel baseball, basketball, and youth football up through junior high school. He was almost always on good teams, started, and played well. But as the kids grew, Isaiah became more noticeably undersized, especially for basketball and football. Entering into his freshman year at one of the biggest and most successful high schools in the state of Michigan, Detroit Catholic Central, Isaiah was just over 5' tall and about 95 pounds. The freshman football team had 72 players, almost all bigger and stronger. That season, Isaiah saw only a couple minutes of late-game action the entire year, which was a humbling experience. He then went out for the freshmen basketball team, probably his best sport at the time, with about 45 other kids trying out for 15 spots. Isaiah was the smallest of the 45 freshmen trying out for the team and admittedly a bit intimidated. He made it until the final tryout practice and was one of the last couple kids cut from the team.

I remember the day he was cut. My wife called me at work. It was a hard experience for all of us, his mother who just wanted him to be able to enjoy the sports he loved, his brother who was doing quite well in soccer, and for me, his former youth sports coach and dad who also wanted him to be happy playing what he enjoyed playing. When I came home from work that day, my wife whispered that he was up in his room. So I walked up slowly, wondering if I had sent him to the right high school; maybe a smaller high school would have been better for his confidence and success. I approached his door, quietly. I slowly opened the door to see him lying still on his bed looking up at the ceiling. He said, "hi dad," in a sort of matter-of-fact way. I didn't know what to say. I asked him how he was doing. He said, "fine." He wasn't crying. He was calm. I told him I was sorry to hear the bad news, but was proud of him giving it his best. I then asked him what he might want to do next. He immediately responded, "I think I'm going to wrestle." I paused. I was surprised at his comment since Isaiah had never wrestled in his life and since Detroit Catholic Central was arguably the best wrestling program in Michigan and arguably one of the best in the midwest and among the better programs in the country. I remember being so impressed that he had already moved on from his disappointment and was not only thinking about next steps but seemed to have already thought it through and decided to give wrestling a try. From that moment, Isaiah wrestled for two years in a fantastic program that developed him physically and mentally. He had some early success, even pinning a couple guys in his first few matches, but then got "stuck" (as those wrestlers call getting pinned) multiple times himself — both were excellent for his development. His coaches in wrestling, especially the outstanding varsity coach

Mitch Hancock and JV coach Mike Carrier, taught Isaiah not only how to wrestle, but how to workout hard, to be mentally strong, to overcome all challenges, to get up every time you get knocked down, and to know that you probably have more in your tank — to even run sprints after every match, win or lose. Isaiah still played football, but still struggled for a couple years to see any significant action. But he kept working hard. He didn't lose his enthusiasm for his favorite sport, football. About this time, I stumbled on a note that Isaiah wrote to himself that said:

"For some, size gives them an automatic chance. For others, size makes them work harder."

By his senior year in football, when his team was undefeated under the legendary high school football coach Tom Mach, Isaiah finally got his chance to shine. The perennial power football program, known for its basic disciplined running attack, opened up their offense a bit mid-way through the year and went to the air, passing the ball more than they had done in years. Isaiah emerged as a weapon as a receiver. His first catch, a simple 5-yard hitch route and short catch, was followed by a quick spin, leaving a falling defender behind, a sprint up the sideline and a dive to the corner pylon for a 55 yard touchdown. Many of our own fans didn't even know his name yet at that point of the year. Later in the season, in the state quarterfinals, Isaiah scored the opening TD and caught 6 passes in the first half alone. And now he is playing college football for the Northern Michigan University Wildcats. But this story is not about accomplishments alone, but instead about a player and person who has never let his obstacles prevent him from maintaining his passion, working hard, never giving up, maintaining a positive attitude, not blaming others, looking forward to better things to come, and delivering when he got his chance. He is mastering adversity.

Reflections After Falling Short

In 1987, in the NCAA Division II National Football Semi-finals, in Portland, Oregon, the Northern Michigan University Wildcats were Playing Portland State University. The winner would go to the national championship. Picture me as the quarterback for the Wildcats late in the 4th quarter, down by one touchdown. I had broken my ankle (spiral fracture) in the third quarter, but was in no way going to leave that game as a senior. I kept playing, trying to lead my team to the comeback victory. That's the seemingly heroic part of my story. However, it does not end heroically. As I hobbled onto the field for our final two series, I recall the frustration of not having the ability to run or move as I needed to. I recall not having the swagger, the confidence and ability to handle pressure that I took pride in up to that point during the season. I was distracted by my injury and allowed a bit of panic to set in and proceeded to throw two interceptions in the final two series, which sealed our loss, ended our glorious season, and closed the door on my football career. I allowed the injury and my emotions to impair my judgement. I did not master adversity in that situation and I let my team down.

As I reflect on my personal situation, I think about a much more well-known athlete and athletic achievement from the 1996 Olympics. The USA gymnastics team was at the brink of losing their lead in the team competition over the best in the world and needed a 9.430 or better on the final exercise, the vault, to win gold. They were down to their last gymnast, a small 18 year old named Kerri Strug who had two attempts to clinch first place and the gold medal for Team USA. She was healthy and confident in her first attempt, but landed awkwardly and fell to the floor in pain. Not only did she not achieve the required score of 9.430, but she tore two ligaments in her ankle as a result of the poor landing. But instead of allowing this serious injury to stop her, instead of allowing this injury to prevent her team from winning gold, instead of allowing her injury take her focus away from her final vault, she somehow managed to focus on the mechanics of her final attempt. She sprinted down the runway, sprung off of the board, flipped and spun, and stuck the landing to clinch the gold medal for her team and her country. As she was carried off of the floor and the score was read, her tears of pain became mixed with tears of joy. As I heard one reporter say it years later, the pain was temporary, but the pride is forever. That was not only dealing with adversity, but mastering adversity.

I wish I could live my final football game again. But I knew the minute after the game was over that I would never get that chance to relive that moment and make better decisions, to throw the ball away instead of throwing a "prayer." What a powerful, painful lesson for me. However, just as I'm trying to do for you in this book, I know that I became a stronger person after that experience, after reflecting on how I might have handled it differently, watching how others have mastered adversity, and then vowing to become even better at handling adversity as I moved on with my life.

Psychologists call this ability to learn from going through adversity as 'post-traumatic growth' and they see people emerge from difficult times feeling stronger and more confident. Some even feel that their lives have new meaning. By enduring trauma or adversity such as the loss of a loved one, a natural disaster, or serious illness or injury, they build confidence for handling future adversity and for new ventures in their lives.[4]

Master Adversity in Workplace and Career

Just like losses and failure are a normal part of athletics, the workplace is full of quality issues, customer concerns, lay-offs, financial losses, and workplace stress. Failure is a part of success. Problems are normal. There is much more to mastering adversity than simply getting through business problems such as these. Failure, mistakes, and problems can be good or bad — but they are only good if we learn from them, adjust quickly, and get better as a result.

90 - 10 Rule

I've worked with too may people who focus the majority of their energy and attention on what is going wrong rather than on *what is working well* and what can be done *to get even better*. These people are the ones that make it hard as a team to master adversity. They are like ankle weights for a runner.

Mastering adversity is not about ignoring problems. You must always be clear about the problems you are facing. But it *is*

---

[4] https://www.wsj.com/articles/after-a-hurricane-new-confidence-1506350306?mod=e2fb

about focusing only about 10% of your time and energy on what is wrong or what went wrong and spending 90+% of your time and energy on what you're going to do about it, the potential solutions, and then actually doing something to address the problems and implement the solutions.

Bill Campbell - from Football Coach to "Trillion Dollar" Leadership Coach

Bill Campbell was an undersized football lineman in college and later became a college football coach with limited success. However, he took the tools he developed in football — discipline as a habit, coaching skills, great teammate, hard work, etc. — and took a shot in the 1980s at some crazy new software companies in Silicon Valley. By the end of his career, he became one of the most successful business people and executive coaches in history. Two of the companies for which he coached their top leaders in the early start-up days, Apple and Google, achieved a market capitalization of more than a trillion dollars. Bill was notorious for challenging leaders to lead. Especially when faced with adversity, Bill would strongly encourage leaders to show even more loyalty, commitment, and decisiveness to the people who were in need of their leadership.[5]

Beware of Extremist Language

Among my work colleagues, I became known as being on guard for and calling out what I refer to as *"extremist language"*

---

[5] Trillion Dollar Coach: The Leadership Playbook of Silicon Valley's Bill Campbell, Eric Schmidt, Jonathan Rosenberg, Alan Eagle

when times start getting difficult. In the workplace, words like "everybody", "always", "never", and "nobody." Phrases like, "nobody ever cares about…", "everybody always tries to….", "they all think that we always ….", you probably get the point. Extremist language is a warning sign that somebody may not be helping the team master adversity, but is allowing their emotions around the adversity to knock them off balance and prevent at least some of their rational thinking. They are likely exaggerating a situation out of fear, anger, or some other type of anxiety or ulterior motive. Management, for example, may be criticized by their employees as "never caring about any of the workers" when making a policy change. Or employees may be criticized by a frustrated management as "always wanting way more than they deserve." Neither of these statements are true in almost all companies. And not only is the extremist language most often not accurate, when used, it generally rubs some other person or group the wrong way. As a result, the words add to the already heightened state of emotion in the midst of adversity and further separates individuals or groups. In the example above that characterizes the feelings of management and employees, you can see how those statements could easily ratchet up the emotion further in the wrong direction between those employees and their management.

So an important part of mastering adversity is to be aware of when the adversity is getting the best of your emotions and those of others. Extremist language is both an indicator that you are probably not mastering adversity and an opportunity to better manage your emotions and then be able to make rational decisions. Is saying "often" or "at this time" more accurate and less abrasive than saying "always"? Is using "not at this time" or "rarely" more appropriate and more productive than using "never"? Words matter, and the ability to maintain composure and be able to select the right phrases in the heat of a battle is a powerful tool in mastering adversity and conflict.

Master Adversity in the Family

Researchers have studied families for many years. The Family Strengths Model, based on research beginning in the 1980s considered clusters of qualities that describe strong families, including:

> *Successful management of stress and crisis. Strong families are not immune to stress and crisis, but they are not as crisis-prone as troubled families tend to be. Rather, they possess the ability to manage both daily stressors and difficult life crises creatively and effectively. They know how to prevent trouble before it happens, and how to work together to meet the inevitable challenges when they occur.[6]*

Researchers looking at families from a strengths perspective have developed a number of propositions taken from their studies with families, including:

- Crises can tear families apart. Crises can also make family relationships stronger. Families in crisis sometimes forget their strengths, and need to remind themselves.

---

[6] John DeFrain and Nick Stinnett

- A family's strengths are the foundation for growth and positive change. Families become stronger by capitalizing on their strengths.

- Most families in the world have considerable strength. Human beings would not have lasted across countless generations without these qualities. There are many more strong families in the world than families who are deeply troubled. As a global human community, we cannot afford to forget this.

- Families are about strong emotion. If family strengths could be reduced to one single quality, it would be the positive emotional connection and sense of belonging with each other. When this emotional bond is present, the family can endure most any hardship.[7]

So a family's ability to master adversity *when* (not if) it occurs will dictate how well it will endure as a family and how well it will support each member of the family.

Too Strong

One of my best friends of all time and my former college football teammate, Brian Franks, is a super hero when it comes to leading a family through adversity. Brian was an all region (upper peninsula of Michigan) dream team, all-state and Hall-of-Fame offensive linemen from Escanaba, Michigan. Brian later became the leader of the NMU offensive line during some of the most prolific running

---

[7] https://www.encyclopedia.com/reference/encyclopedias-almanacs-transcripts-and-maps/family-strengths

attacks in Wildcat football history, earning him all conference (Great Lakes Intercollegiate Athletic Conference) first team and most valuable lineman honors. Brian was a critical senior leader on the 1987 undefeated GLIAC champions and #1 ranked NCAA Division II football team in the nation. He was a truly great football player, leader and teammate. Through athletics, Brian was preparing for the ultimate challenge of his life.

In 2009, Brian was first diagnosed with cancer and began a journey of battling this horrible disease. For the next nine years, Brian endured several major surgeries, years of chemotherapy, and countless efforts undergoing experimental procedures and medications to try and hold off the effects of this mysterious and deadly disease. Throughout this time, as he physically deteriorated, Brian continued to be an amazing father, devoted husband and special friend. He somehow managed to continue to be a highly successful business person, despite the tremendous physical and emotional hardships he faced. And although he had every right to be down, angry, and focused on himself, he was the opposite — always sharing a smile or a joke, upbeat and more concerned about his beautiful wife Ann, his amazing children, Zach, Abby, and Grace, his parents, brothers and even his goofball NMU Wildcat football friends, than he was concerned about himself.

As the family battled Brian's cancer along his side, they developed a mantra or rallying cry, "Too Strong." Brian was quite simply Too Strong to let anything prevent him from being the man he was intended to be and to make those around him better by his presence.

On February 21, 2018, Brian left this earth. At his memorial, on a card bearing Brian's picture with his usual smile, he left us with two quotes that summed up Brian's attitude toward his 9-year battle with this horrible disease:

> *First, quoting the late great NC State Basketball Coach Jim Valvano: "Cancer can take away all my physical abilities. It cannot touch my mind, it cannot touch my heart and it cannot touch my soul. And those three things are going to carry on forever."*

> *And from the late great ESPN Announcer, Stuart Scott: "When you die, it does not mean that you lose to cancer, you beat cancer by how you live, why you live and in the manner which you live."*

I pray that no family has to go through what Brian and his family endured, but whenever a family is faced with adversity, they can look to Brian as the consummate role model for leading a family through and mastering adversity.

Adversity Across Athletics, Workplace, and Family

Looking across athletics, workplace & career, and family life, let me recap how to master adversity in a succinct summary:

Preparation (*Before Adversity*): Recognize that adversity is a part of your sport, career, family, and life. Prepare yourself physically, mentally, and emotionally for when (not if) problems and challenges arise.

Response (*During Adversity*): Attack the challenges head-on, don't avoid them, and be aware of your physical, mental, and emotional reaction to the challenges. Maintain your composure, keep your cool. Take control of the situation. Force big picture thinking while you decide on specific immediate actions. Do the right things, uphold your and your team/company/family values.

Reflection *(After Adversity):* Learn from every experience with adversity. How did you do? Did you allow emotion to block your rational thinking? Did you attack the adversity head on and with confidence? Did you focus on solutions instead of dwelling on problems? Did you make good decisions? Did you uphold your values? How did you treat people? How can you be even better next time?

Mastering COVID-19 Pandemic

With these 3 phases in mind, let's reflect on one the greatest challenges of our lifetimes, a timely and significant experience with adversity — the Coronavirus pandemic of 2020.

Preparation - Before COVID-19

Did you or most people recognize that a pandemic like coronavirus could emerge? Were you (or others) physically, mentally, and emotionally prepared for a challenge like coronavirus?

I believe the answer to these questions for the most part is "no." Although vast numbers of people were vaguely aware that a pandemic *could* occur, a pandemic certainly was viewed as *not likely to occur* by most people in this modern era. Again, many people were aware that pandemics have occurred in our history, such as long ago in 1346-1353, when the Bubonic

Plague killed 75-200 million people in Europe, Africa, and Asia, or the Flu Pandemic of 1918, called the Spanish Flu, resulted in the death of 20-50 million people, or the Asian Flu of 1956-1958 which was responsible for about 2 million deaths, the Flu Pandemic of 1968, sometimes called "the Hong Kong Flu" which killed more than 1 million people. And even more people were aware of the recent HIV/AIDS pandemic, which was at its peak in 2005-2012, and has killed 36 million people globally since 1981. Several other pandemics and epidemics have taken place throughout history, including recent history. So a pandemic is something that has been a known possibility for a long time. Experts on contagious diseases were aware that this was a real possibility, but the general public was quite certainly not as aware as the experts, and most of us didn't expect anything like the coronavirus experience to happen to us as it did. So, in general, I do not believe that we as a society acknowledged a global pandemic as a legitimate possibility.

Were we physically, mentally, and emotionally prepared?

This question has millions of answers. Unfortunately, those with pre-existing health problems were most at risk of serious illness; they were less physically prepared to handle this type of adversity. Most people would be quick to agree that being healthy in general will prevent disease more than being unhealthy. For most, living a healthy lifestyle is a choice. For some, bad health is simply bad luck. But choosing a healthy lifestyle is a fundamentally smart way to prepare physically for almost any adversity, especially for a contagious disease.

But the more fascinating part of watching this pandemic unfold for me was observing the mental and emotional preparedness (or lack thereof) to master the adversity of a pandemic. Many were simply not ready to deal with the coronavirus pandemic, neither mentally nor emotionally, as evidenced by their responses.

Response - In the Middle of COVID-19

How did you respond? How did others respond? Were you aware of your emotions and subsequent reactions? Did you take control of your reactions? Did you manage yourself and help others get through this adversity in a productive way?

Every person had their own experience with the pandemic. Some ran out and bought months supply of toilet paper. Others hurried to buy handguns and alcohol. Some didn't heed the warnings and direction from their public leaders, such as the Spring Break partiers in Florida who continued to expose themselves and then others to the virus in the earliest days when very little was known about it. Their ignorance of the both the realities of what was happening (mental unpreparedness) and their arrogance made them believe they were in fact mastering adversity (emotional unpreparedness). However, given the lack of knowledge of the virus at that time, their disregard serves as a what-not-to-do in the midst of adversity.

As evidenced and highlighted in social media, many people allowed fear to get the best of them. Their reactions included anger, hate, and lashing out at whomever they could blame and ridicule for their fear, inconvenience, or even their sickness. We saw the politicization of a non-partisan issue, incongruent policy decisions and directives, by politicians from all parties, which threw gasoline on the fires of blame and hate by their avid followers and their opposition.

However, at the same time, we saw heroic individuals step up to help others, especially in the healthcare field, seeing people risking their own health to help others who were sick. We also saw heroism in the jobs we rarely notice or job we take for granted, like grocery store workers, and cleaners. We saw many social media posts of people being creative while at home, sharing humorous video skits to cheer up their friends, and setting a positive example for their children. We saw some politicians set aside partisan differences to focus on resolving the shortage of protective equipment and making public funds available for people most impacted. Those mentally and emotionally prepared were smart with their comments and actions. They not only kept their composure but they also maintained their sense of humor and focus on others.

Reflection - Looking Back at COVID-19

The final phase of mastering adversity, after the storm has slowed or the heat of the battle has passed, is to reflect on how you managed the challenge.

How did you handle COVID-19 pandemic? Did you do your part to be safe for yourself and others? Did you run for cartons of toilet paper, multiple guns, or other panic purchases? Did you step up to help others? Did you pay attention to what was happening and continually become better educated on the challenge and the effectiveness of your reaction to the challenge? Did you maintain a positive attitude and bring people up and toward success? Or did you fall into blaming, panicking, hating, or otherwise negatively impacting the situation and others? Did you learn from others who seemed to manage the adversity well? What did others do differently than you that you can learn from?

Take some time to think through this example or any other recent example of how you were faced with adversity. Take what you did well and where you could have done better, and get ready for the next one. It will come sooner or later.

As Best Selling Author and Keynote Speaker Jon Gordon nicely summarized in the midst of the early part of the COVID-19 pandemic,

> *"We've been hit by a massive wave of change. For most of us it is not a year that we are thinking about thriving. For many we are just trying to keep our head above water, pay our bills, feed our family, teach our kids, keep our homes, deal with the fear and anxiety, stay healthy and make it to another day. In this spirit, let's look at the ocean of possibilities and maintain optimism and hope. Optimism is not a supplemental way to think. It's an essential way to think to overcome adversity and waves of change. Let's look for ways to survive and be creative and innovative so we can advance and adapt that will allow us to thrive once again in the future. Through this process when we look back on this time we'll learn that surviving allowed us to advance, our discomfort led to our growth, the change made us adapt, and adapting made us stronger which helped us thrive as a result."*

Timeless Poem

I close this chapter with one of the greatest poems ever written, an oldie but a true classic. And although it is written from a father to a son, the spirit and message equally applies to mothers, daughters, and any coaching or mentoring relationship with young people.

"IF" by Rudyard Kipling

If you can keep your head when all about you
Are losing theirs and blaming it on you,
If you can trust yourself when all men doubt you,
But make allowance for their doubting too;
If you can wait and not be tired by waiting,
Or being lied about, don't deal in lies,
Or being hated, don't give way to hating,
And yet don't look too good, nor talk too wise:

If you can dream—and not make dreams your master;
If you can think—and not make thoughts your aim;
If you can meet with Triumph and Disaster
And treat those two impostors just the same;
If you can bear to hear the truth you've spoken
Twisted by knaves to make a trap for fools,
Or watch the things you gave your life to, broken,
And stoop and build 'em up with worn-out tools:

If you can make one heap of all your winnings
And risk it on one turn of pitch-and-toss,
And lose, and start again at your beginnings
And never breathe a word about your loss;

If you can force your heart and nerve and sinew
To serve your turn long after they are gone,
And so hold on when there is nothing in you
Except the Will which says to them: 'Hold on!'

If you can talk with crowds and keep your virtue,
Or walk with Kings—nor lose the common touch,
If neither foes nor loving friends can hurt you,
If all men count with you, but none too much;
If you can fill the unforgiving minute
With sixty seconds' worth of distance run,
Yours is the Earth and everything that's in it,
And—which is more—you'll be a Man, my son!

Thought Leaders and Role Models on Mastering Adversity

"Adversity introduces a man to himself."

— Albert Einstein,
often considered as one of the smartest people in history

"Strength does not come from winning. Your struggles develop your strengths. When you go through hardships and decide not to surrender, that is strength."

— Mahatma Gandhi,
one of histories greatest leaders from India

"All the adversity I've had in my life, all my troubles and obstacles, have strengthened me. You may not realize it when it happens, but a kick in the teeth may be the best things in the world for you."

— well-known animator and entrepreneur **Walt Disney**

"Tough times don't last, tough people do."

— my former college football coach,
Herb Grenke, Northern Michigan University used to frequently use this powerful phrase from Christian evangelist **Robert Schuller**

"You can't give up! If you give up, you're like everybody else."

– Chris Evert,

retired American World No. 1 tennis player, business person, and ESPN tennis analyst & commentator. She won 18 Grand Slam singles championships and three doubles titles. She was the year-ending World No. 1 singles player in 1974, 1975, 1976, 1977, 1978, 1980, and 1981.

"We all have obstacles. The feeling of satisfaction comes by overcoming something."

– Marta Vieira da Silva,

Brazilian soccer star, considered by many as the world's best female soccer player

"Optimism is the faith that leads to achievement."

– Helen Keller,

an American author, political activist and campaigner for deaf and blind charities. She became deaf and blind as a young child yet became the first deaf-blind person to attain a bachelor's degree and became an influential campaigner for social, political and disability issues.

Your Choice: Will you Master Adversity?

Lesson #5: Peak Performance State

Are you putting yourself and keeping yourself in the best position for top performance:

1) Mentally?

2) Physically?

3) Emotionally?

Peak Performance State in the Athletics

Mentally: Do you know your position inside and out? The game-plan? Your assignments? Your opponent's tendencies? Do you study your sport? Do you watch videos of the best who play your sport? Do you watch videos of your own performance, in practice and in games? Do you watch videos of your opponents performance? Have you become a student of your sport?

Physically: Are you physically capable of playing your position well? Doing your job well? Do you get enough sleep, eat appropriately, workout according to what your position needs? Are you physically skilled enough to be excellent at your position or job, to give consistently high levels of performance? Do you have the physical endurance to play at the top of your game for the entire game?

Emotionally: Do you have high emotional intelligence to know what to expect in your game and to deal with the ups and downs, the pressure situations? Are you mentally tough enough to handle the successes and failures of a game, a season, and continue to manage those situations effectively? Do you have the grit to endure discomfort, pain, or injury to achieve tough goals? Are you enthusiastic and one that brings others up, especially when times are tough?

Kobe Bryant at Peak Performance State

We recently experienced the loss of the legendary basketball star Kobe Bryant, along with his beautiful young daughter Gianna, and seven of their friends to a tragic helicopter accident. As the world mourned this tragic incident, many stories were shared in honor of Kobe's work ethic, physical conditioning, study of the game of basketball, his ever-curious mind, and his *mamba mentality.*

Kobe retired from professional basketball as a five-time NBA champion with two NBA Finals MVPs, a Most Valuable Player, an 18-time NBA All-Star, four-time NBA All-Star Game MVP, 11-time All-NBA First Team, two-time All-NBA Second Team, two-time All-NBA Third Team, nine-time NBA All-Defensive First Team, three-time NBA All-Defensive Second Team, two-time NBA scoring champion, an NBA Slam Dunk Contest champion, made it to the NBA All-Rookie Second Team, became the Naismith Prep Player of the Year, and a First-Team Parade All-American. He ended with 33,643 points, 7,047 rebounds, 6,306 assists, an incredible 81-point game that may have been the greatest offensive performance in NBA history, and a 61-point outing in his final game before retirement.

In light of all of this success and sudden tragic end, the public got to see more of what went into making Kobe Bryant so successful, including these stories about Kobe:[8]

- He used to show up for 7 am practice at 5 am...in high school (sports illustrated)

- He would force his high school teammates to play 1-on-1 games to 100 (SI)

- He used to watch films of himself at halftime (ESPN)

- Former Lakers player and head coach Byron Scott said he once found an 18-year-old Bryant shooting in a dark gym two hours before practice.

- Former NBA player and Lakers teammate John Celestand said Kobe was always the first player in the gym, even when he was hurt.

- He once played left-handed because he injured his right shoulder.

- Former teammate Shaquille O'Neal said Kobe used to practice without a ball.

- He decided to lose 16 pounds for the Olympics in 2012, citing the need to keep his knees pain-free. (Guardian)

- According to a trainer from the olympic Team USA trainer, Kobe once held a workout from 4:15 a.m. to

[8] Scott Davis and Connor Perrett in their Jan 26, 2020 article in Business Insider

11 a.m., refusing to leave the gym until he made 800 shots. (Ball is Life)

■ He was strict about what he ate, eliminating sugar and pizza and eating only lean meat. (ESPN)

In his book entitled, *'Mamba Mentality: How I Play'* Kobe Bryant captured his mental and emotional approach to basketball, which he later applied to his life off the court. In the book, Kobe, also known as "The Black Mamba," shared his vast knowledge and understanding of the game of basketball and the core elements of his legendary "Mamba mentality."

> *"Mamba mentality is all about focusing on the process and trusting in the hard work when it matters most," he told Amazon Book Review. "It's the ultimate mantra for the competitive spirit. It started just as a hashtag that came to me one day, and it's grown into something athletes — and even non-athletes — embrace as a mindset."*

> *"Hard work outweighs talent — every time," he continued. "Mamba mentality is about 4 a.m. workouts, doing more than the next guy and then trusting in the work you've put in when it's time to perform. Without studying, preparation and practice, you're leaving the outcome to fate. I don't do fate."* [9]

Other Role Model Athletes for Peak Performance State

The sports world is full of role models who get themselves into peak performance condition, physically, mentally, and

---

[9] Christina Montford, January 31, 2020, Showbiz CheatSheet.com

emotionally. For young athletes, I encourage you to take full advantage of your athletic preparation experience by learning from some of these role models. They can teach you and inspire you to best prepare for your sport, which will then carry over into preparing for the other roles that you play in your life.

Here are only a couple to consider watching closely.

JJ Watt

An athlete with a legendary reputation for getting himself into peak performance state and maintaining that ultimate level of preparedness, mentally, physically, and emotionally. JJ Watt, has been the NFL Defensive Player of the Year, one of the few to win the award multiple times and named to the top spot in the NFL Top 100 Players of 2015. Just a quick rundown of his approach to being in peak performance state:

- Has become an expert in his position requirements, physical development, and emotional state of mind.

- Eats a massive amount of healthy food each day. So much so, he considers eating to be a chore.

- Loves to work out. Every aspect, from foam rolling to muscle activation drills, he's enthusiastic about. Watt does many of the same routines he has since high school,

- Highly tuned to what his body tells him and is constantly adjusting to make things work at their optimum level. Watt can flip a 1000-lb. tractor tire, bench 225-lb. 34 times and squat 700+ lbs. He also has a 61 inch vertical box jump.

- Training sessions last 90 minutes. He starts out by stretching on the foam roller, then moves on to footwork and does a lot with resistance bands.

- Makes sure to give time to stretching and recovery so that he's in top form at all times.

- Dedicated to his profession, physically and mentally. In his words, "Right now, I am a football player and will sacrifice whatever is necessary to be the best." [10]

Giannis Antetokounmpo, NBA Milwaukee Bucks

In his first year in the league, Giannis Antetokounmpo was 6'9" and 196 pounds—no doubt a towering figure in any sport. But since then, the Milwaukee Bucks star added a few inches and bulked up his already-intimidating frame to a menacing 6'11" and 242 pounds, with a 7'3" wingspan, a testament to his commitment to overall fitness and conditioning for the rigors of the NBA. In this past season, Antetokounmpo improved in nearly every aspect of the game, from three-point shooting to usage rate, assists and more. He can score in the paint, he can sink shots from the outside and he's a dynamic playmaker, which is why the 25-year-old is consistently in the running to win another MVP award. Although Giannis has clearly been gifted with natural abilities,

---

[10] source: https://fitnessclone.com/jj-watt/

his work ethic and commitment to continually improving is what has earned him the nickname "Greek Freak." [11]

In Giannis' words, "It's very important for me to never stop improving, even in the offseason. When I'm not on the court playing I'm in the gym training and building strength. There is no time off. Eating well and exercising right is very important to me."[12]

Simone Biles, Olympic Gymnastic Champion

For multiple years, Sports Illustrated has named Simone Biles as the most fit professional athlete in the world. At age 22, Simone is already the most dominant gymnast ever, and though she stands at just 4'9", she continues to eclipse the competition and push the limits of her sport. Biles will take the stage at the Tokyo 2020 Games, hoping to add to her four gold medals from Rio 2016, after spending 2019 crushing more records and raking in even more hardware, winning five more gold medals at the 2019 World Championships to become the most decorated gymnast ever, with 25 medals total. Biles's mastery of the vault, balance beam, floor exercise and more demonstrate the diversity of her conditioning, power, flexibility and strength. There's no denying that Biles work ethic is keeping her as a top all-around athlete in every aspect of the word.[13]

---

[11] https://www.si.com/edge/2020/02/06/fittest-50-2020

[12] https://fit.nba.com/qa-with-giannis-antetokounmpo/

[13] https://www.si.com/edge/2020/02/06/fittest-50-2020

Mikaela Shiffrin, Alpine Skiing

The list of accolades for Mikaela Shiffrin is lengthy: the youngest slalom champion in Olympic history; the youngest skier to earn 50 World Cup race wins; the first skier—of any gender—to earn $1 million in prize money in a single season; 66 (and counting) World Cup victories ... and so on. So, it should come as no surprise that the 24-year-old is disciplined and regimented when it comes to her training, keeping detailed data logs, prioritizing sleep and hitting the gym as hard as she hits the slopes. Sports Illustrated picked Mikaela as one of the world's most fit athletes in 2020.[14]

Peyton Manning, NFL Quarterback

Fourteen NFL Pro Bowl appearances, five-time NFL MVP, has played in four Super Bowls and has won two. Though Peyton has a tremendous throwing skills, he is not known particularly for his physical strength, speed, or condition. Instead, he has become even more well known for his intense preparation for each game, mentally and emotionally, including analyzing hours of game film and being able to remain cool under immense pressure. In his own words from a speech to a business group, he said:

> "At some point you are going to have to come from behind," Manning said. "When that happens, my advice is to play smart, not scared. How? By relentless preparation. I never left a field feeling I could have done more to prepare myself, regardless of the outcome. The teams I

---

[14] https://www.si.com/edge/2020/02/06/fittest-50-2020

was on, our best players were our best practicers. Preparation was where I always thought I could get an edge. I couldn't out throw anybody, I certainly couldn't outrun anybody, but I could out-prepare others. Ask yourself, what are you willing to do to be a better leader, better organization?"15

Prepare Like the Best in Athletics

As an athlete, my advice to you is to pick one or two of your favorite athletes, the ones you admire in your sport and as a personal role model. Study their approach to the physical, mental, and emotional aspects of your sport. Learn from them. And get yourself into your own peak performance state.

Peak Performance State in the Workplace and Career

To attain and maintain the peak performance state in your job and career, challenge yourself in the same three categories, but with slightly different questions and considerations:

Mentally: Constantly educate yourself about your line of work. In your job, do you know your objectives, business plan, competitors, and industry trends? Do you study your profession? Do you read about the best in your line of work? Do you conduct "after action reviews" of your work products? Have you become a student of your profession?

---

15 https://www.cutoday.info/THE-feature/Peyton-Manning-Puts-Premium-on-Preparation

Physically: Are you physically capable of doing your job well? Do you get enough sleep, eat appropriately, workout according to your physical job requirements? Are you physically skilled enough to be excellent at your job, to give consistently high levels of performance?

Emotionally: Do you have high emotional intelligence to know what to expect in your job, your company? Are you mentally tough enough to handle the potential ups and downs of your line of work and of the industry in which you work? Do you have grit to endure hard-work, pay your dues, and sacrifice to achieve tough business goals? Are you enthusiastic and one who brings others up, especially when times are tough?

I mentioned Kobe Bryant with respect to his approach to athletics, yet after he retired from playing basketball, he continued to deploy that same work ethic, mental preparation, and emotional tenacity that he developed in athletics to achieve success in business. A few more stories from Kobe's approach to business:[16]

- Billionaire investor Chris Sacca said Kobe was relentless in learning more about investing after Sacca told him to do his homework. Sacca told Bill Simmons, host of the Bill Simmons podcast, "For the next few months my phone never stops buzzing in the middle of the night. It's Kobe, reading this article, checking out this tweet, following this guy, diving into this Ted Talk, diving into the Y Combinator Demo

---

[16] Scott Davis and Connor Perrett from Business Insider

Day stuff. And I'm getting these texts, literally two or three in the morning, and my wife is like, 'Are you having an affair with Kobe Bryant? What is happening here?"(Source: Bill Simmons podcast)

- He texted business leaders at all hours of the day, including 3 a.m., to pick their brains. (ESPN)

- He cold-called business people and entrepreneurs to learn more about them and the secrets to success. (Bloomberg)

- When talking about how he wanted to be remembered, Kobe said, "To think of me as a person that's overachieved, that would mean a lot to me. That means I put a lot of work in and squeezed every ounce of juice out of this orange that I could." (Yahoo)

Learning in Flint and Applying at Google

A friend of mine, Chip Grimes, grew up in the Flint, Michigan, area which was known especially at his time growing up as a hotbed for athletes and competitive sports. Some of the best high school, college, and professional athletes have come out of Flint. Chip was driven by competitive athletics as a young man, has since become a highly successful business person, is now an executive at Google, and is actively involved with his wonderful family. As he reflects back on his early days, he shares with us, "Growing up, sports was a big driver of my life. I knew early I wasn't the most talented athlete in the greater Flint area, however I wanted to have success. Therefore, hard work was a must.

With early hours at the gym and late evenings, I felt I could get ahead. Plus I had to work on the areas to improve beside athleticism, understanding situations, knowing your opponent, knowing your team strengths: all of this transferred to the real world." In other words, Chip recognized early on that he had to attain and maintain his peak performance state, physically, mentally, and emotionally in order to compete at the highest levels in athletics as a youngster and later in the business world as he continues to do today.

Prepare Like the Best in the Workplace

As with athletics, find the best people in your line of work and learn how they prepare, mentally, physically, and emotionally. In my case, I have several role models in the type of work that I do, including people like author and speaker Patrick Lencioni, who I referenced earlier in this book, the late Bill Campbell, known as the 'Trillion Dollar Coach,' Alan Mulally, the former CEO of Ford Motor Company, Bill Ford, Jr., Executive Chairperson of Ford, and several of my former business partners, bosses, and other leaders at Ford Motor Company. There is always more you can learn from people who do what you do extremely well and who also display the type of character that you admire.

Peak Performance State in the Family

To attain and maintain the peak performance state in your family, again, challenge yourself in the same three categories, with slightly different questions once more:

Mentally: Do you think about what it takes to make a great family? Do you read or listen to experts or role-models on family relationships and strong families? Do you know what the rest of your family thinks about what it takes to have a great family?

Physically: Do you keep yourself healthy and encourage your family members to stay healthy? So often, health problems cause family problems. Too often, for example, health care expenses disrupt and even destroy the financial well-being of a family, which then tears down family relationships. Some health care issues are simply bad luck, but more are the result of unhealthy habits over time. Are you a positive influence on the physical health of your family?

Emotionally: Do you have high emotional intelligence to most effectively contribute to an emotionally healthy family? Do you have emotional discipline to avoid sibling arguments or fighting with parents who are trying to help you? Do you have the ability to delay the satisfaction of "fun" in order to help out around your house? Are you enthusiastic and one who brings others up, especially when times are tough in the family? Do you show empathy for other family members?

Closing out the Kobe Bryant example of maintaining peak performance state in athletics, workplace, and family, Newsweek Magazine published a January 2020 article by Jordan Harbinger, who interviewed Kobe only months before his death. In the article, Harbinger shared Kobe's perspective on "setting examples" as a parent. Bryant said:

You can't talk your children into working hard. That's the one thing that drives me crazy, [when] parents come up to me on the street or when I'm at the sports academy [the Mamba Sports Academy, Bryant's joint-venture training facility] and say, OK, how can I get my kid to work hard, what do I need to tell them? Can you talk to my kid? I say, listen, it's not something that you can talk through. It's a behavioral thing: you have to get up every day and do the work. Consistently do the work.

My kids' volleyball, basketball, school work—they work every day, and that's how you instill it in them, where it becomes a behavioral thing and it doesn't matter what they decide to do [as adults]. Like if Gianna decides to not play basketball when she grows up, it's fine, but she understands the discipline that it takes to work at something every single day. So, whether she wants to be a writer, a director, a doctor, a lawyer, she'll have those characteristics. It's a behavior.

Also, it's [about] observing you [work hard]—and not just me, my wife too. It's her commitment to the children and making sure that they're on point, [on] schedule, [doing their] school work. Everything is sharp, everything is there, every single day, [like] seeing me get up, train and work hard.

Prepare Like the Best for Families

It's more difficult to identify who is "most successful" in families. However, I encourage you to ask friends, their parents, aunts, uncles, grandparents, and others who you know and respect, about their approach to cultivating strong families. Learn something from everybody, whether you learn what seems to work well, and even if you learn what not to do. Treat your families with the importance that it deserves and prepare yourself to be at your best with your families. Avoid giving all of your effort at school, your sports, and in your job only to leave the leftovers for your family — maintain peak performance state with your family too.

Superpower Capability: Emotional Intelligence

Across all aspects of your life, including athletics, career, and family, I strongly encourage you to build your emotional intelligence at the same time as you are building your physical and intellectual capabilities. Allow me to spend just a little time on emotional intelligence, though I will only scratch the surface on this important topic as it relates to achieving and maintain your peak performance state.

Dr. Daniel Goleman is an internationally known and highly regarded psychologist and science journalist. His 1995 book, *Emotional Intelligence* was on The New York Times bestseller list for a year-and-a-half was a best seller in many countries, along with many other awards. Dr. Goleman has written many books and articles since then, including a more recent book, *Leadership: The Power of Emotional Intelligence.*

In simple terms, emotional intelligence is a different way of being smart. According to Goleman's research, the evidence suggests that emotional intelligence is almost twice as important as pure brainpower (also called cognitive ability, IQ) to be successful as an individual, as a part of a team, or as a leader of a team. Emotional intelligence is the ability to identify, understand, and manage both your own emotions and the emotions of others. In other words, it's the ability to make emotions work for you, instead of against you.

When emotional intelligence was first discovered, it helped explained a peculiar finding that was stumping researchers. That strange finding was that in about 70% of the cases, people with average IQ were outperforming those with high IQ (often considered smarter). Emotional intelligence provided what was considered the missing link to explaining workplace success.[17]

Although Dr. Goleman received significant criticism when he first came out with this concept of emotional intelligence, as neuroscience and behavioral sciences progress, these theories continue to gain more support and validation as being an extremely valuable consideration to succeed in the workplace and in the broader society. In his book called, *The Brain and Emotional Intelligence: New Insights*, Goleman explains, "...the states of disengagement (epidemic in some workplaces), and the frazzle from too much stress (also epidemic) both disable the brain's prefrontal zones, the site of comprehension, focus, learning, and creativity. On the other hand...in the zone of flow the brain operates at peak cognitive efficiency, and people perform at their best."

Frazzle is Bad

This state "frazzle" is described as, "...a neural state in which emotional upsurges hamper the workings of the executive center. While we are frazzled, we cannot concentrate or think clearly. That neural truth has direct implications for achieving

---

[17] Emotional Intelligence 2.0, Bradberry & Greaves

the optimal emotional atmosphere both in the classroom and the office."[18] In simpler words, frazzle is basically "stressing out."

Taking it a bit further, Dr. Goleman explains that doing well in school and at work involves the same state of mind, the brain's sweet spot for performance. The biology of anxiety or stress kicks us out of that sweet spot for excellence. And he further explains how anxiety can crush our ability to perform at our best by saying that the more anxiety we feel, the more impaired is our brain's ability to think efficiently. In this zone of mental misery, we become mentally scattered where distracting thoughts hijack our attention and squeeze our ability and energy to think clearly. Because high anxiety shrinks the space in our brain that is available to our attention, it reduces our very capacity to take in new information, let alone generate fresh ideas. Freaking out (or near-panic as Dr. Goleman calls it) is the enemy of learning and creativity.

Joy is Good

On the brighter side, according to University of Southern California neuroscientist Antonio Damasio, *joyous states of mind* not only enable us to survive the daily grind, but allow us to flourish, to live well, and to feel well-being. Upbeat states of mind, he notes, allow a "greater ease in the capacity to act." He says that the field of cognitive science in studying the neural networks that run mental operations calls these upbeat or joyous states of mind "maximal harmonious states." OK,

---

[18] Academic journal Science referenced in chapter 8 p 104 of Goleman's Leadership, The Power of Emotional Intelligence, collection of articles

maybe we won't use that fancy terminology, but it has been my observation and personal experience over and over again that attaining and maintaining an underlying level of joy, even when things aren't necessarily going our way, enables us to deal with the natural pressures of life, to perform well in our chosen endeavors, to be healthier, and continually grow through new experiences.

Grit is Critical — We Need More Grit

In her book, *Grit: The Power of Passion and Perseverance*, author, researcher, and professor, Angela Duckworth, shares what she believes really drives success. Based on her research including interviews with dozens of high achievers like CEOs of large companies, artists, and NFL coaches, she found that the key driver of success is not genius, but a combination of passion and long-term perseverance. She studied cadets at West Point Military Academy, teachers at some of the toughest schools in America, and the results of modern experiments on peak performance. In all of her work, she narrowed down the key to success, which is she found was what goes through your head when you fall down, and how that—not talent or luck— makes all the difference in achieving success. Those who have developed the ability to persevere through obstacles, pain, failure, and maintain their passion to achieve their goals are far more likely to succeed than those with much more talent. She calls that ability to get back up after falling down, with tenacity and passion, as grit. And the good news is that she also found that grit can be learned.

At the risk of sounding like a crusty old guy, I see a lack of grit today with a continuing declining trend. When I compare the grit of young athletes when I competed versus what I see as I coach today, when I think about my first days in the workplace and compare it with what I saw evolve during my career in human resources in the workplace, when I see how kids and parents manage difficulties in families today versus how families operated as I grew up, and as I continue to research societal and workplace trends and issues, I see a clear drop-off in grit across society in almost all aspects. And I believe that my generation was not nearly as gritty as the ones before mine, especially the "greatest generation," those born between 1901 and 1927, who found themselves not only in the early years of the industrial revolution, but lived through the Great Depression and either fought in or worked to enable victory in World War II and other wars. Through their challenges, in general, that generation simply developed a level of grit unmatched by subsequent generations.

Certainly, statistics will support the increased social issues that exist today with continued troublesome trends. For example, suicide rates in the U.S. have jumped 35% in the past two decades. [19]

I view part of the problem in developed wealthy nations like the U.S. is that instead of honoring, teaching, and encouraging people to develop the ability to cope and to get up after a fall, in other words, instead of cultivating more grit, our society attempts to cushion people from the hardships, opting for explaining and complaining about why the fall happened and whose fault it was. And still others spend their energy on

---

[19] https://www.usnews.com/news/health-news/articles/2020-04-08/us-suicide-rate-climbed-35-37-in-two-decades

explaining that it wasn't even a fall anyway, in order to not hurt anybody's feelings. I'm not saying we have to go back to the days when a coach would say, "tape an aspirin to your leg" when we truly had a leg injury needing medical attention, but some of that mentality sure would help in my view.

Your Own Experience

Stepping away from psychologists, neurologists, researchers, other scientists, and my opinion, you can look at your own experiences when you have been "on a roll" , "in flow" , "having the hot hand", or "being on fire" with your athletic performances. That feeling in basketball when you are "feelin' it," "can't miss," or in golf when you can see and feel the shot before you step up to the ball, or when you "got your touch" in soccer. You have had the feeling of passion and perseverance, the grit to not let anything get in our way. You may also know the opposite feeling of "being off", "not feeling it", "not my day", or the dreaded "choke." You know how it feels to be hurt, afraid, and unmotivated. Having emotional intelligence and continually improving your EQ and your grit will enable you to be more in-flow, on-a-roll, and hot, and be able to get right back up when you fall, rather than out-of-flow, stuck, cold, and ready to give up when times get tough.

Emotional Intelligence is Critical in the Workplace

For many years during my career working in human resources, I held positions responsible for talent management, including performance management, identifying top talent in various organizations, identifying critical characteristics, behaviors, and skills most valuable to the business and to the team. Basic intelligence to perform the job was always critical — that was a given, the minimum requirement to do any job. Certainly, for inexperienced new hires, time is necessary for them to gain the skills and knowledge required to perform their jobs well. And with more time, the job knowledge and skills develop and grow quite naturally for most, with the higher contributors normally being more aggressive in continual learning and skill development. That said, however, as supported by the research, I too found the key difference-maker, the area that enabled certain employees and leaders to stand out from the others, to bring more value to the team and the business, were those with *emotional intelligence.*

There are four parts to Emotional Intelligence model:

- **Self-Awareness:** Do you really know your own emotions? What makes you most angry? What triggers you into bad behavior? What makes you happy? How does stress make you different? How do you handle stress or frazzle?

- **Self-Management:** To what degree do you have emotional self control? When your emotions are triggered, are you able to control your response? Are you adaptable to changing environments and circumstances? Are you achievement oriented? Do you have a positive outlook?

- **Social Awareness:** Do you have and show empathy for others? Are you able to walk in another person's shoes and truly relate to them and their circumstances? Are you aware of the needs of the team and the organization?

- **Relationship Management:** Do you have the ability to influence others? Are you able to coach and mentor others? Are you able to provide inspirational leadership at the appropriate time? Are you comfortable with conflict and able to manage it productively? Are you a great teammate?

According to the experts, within each of these four parts, there are *learned competencies* based on the underlying abilities that make people outstanding in the workplace. The good news is that by saying learned competencies, that means that *these are skills that can be developed.* And just like any other skill, for some, this will come easier than for others. But everybody can build their emotional intelligence.[20]

I could go on for a long time and many more pages on the topic of emotional intelligence, but will close this brief high level overview by strongly encouraging you to study it, make an honest self assessment of your skills in each of the four parts summarized above, and work at developing your emotional intelligence. With high emotional intelligence, you will not only be better able to achieve your peak performance state, but you will also become more coachable and be a better

---

[20] Building Blocks of Emotional Intelligence: Emotional Self-Awareness: A Primer / by Daniel Goleman / Richard Boyatzis / Richard J. Davidson / Vanessa Druskat / George Kohlrieser ISBN 978-1-934441-87-9 Copyright © 2017 by More Than Sound, LLC All Rights Reserved

teammate, two of the lessons already covered. You'll also see that a high EQ will help you in lessons yet to come in the remainder of this book.

Thought Leaders and Role Models on Peak Performance State

"All the physical comes from the mental."

– Clara Hughes,
Canadian cyclist and speed skater who has won multiple Olympic medals in both sports. Hughes won two bronze in the 1996 Summer Olympics and four medals over the course of three Winter Olympics.

"It's not the will to win that matter – everyone has that. It's the will to prepare to win that matters."

– Paul 'Bear' Bryant,
legendary college football coach

"If you prepare yourself at every point as well as you can, with whatever means you may have, however meager they may seem, you will be able to grasp opportunity for broader experience when it appears. Without preparation you cannot do it."

— Eleanor Roosevelt,
political figure, activist, and First Lady to president Franklin D. Roosevelt.

"Emotional intelligence is an extremely important skill to have for personal and professional success."

— **Ken Blanchard,**
best-selling business book author of all time

"Nothing can stop the man with the right mental attitude from achieving his goal; nothing on earth can help the man with the wrong mental attitude."

— **Thomas Jefferson,**
American statesman, diplomat, lawyer, architect, philosopher, and Founding Father who served as the third president of the United States.

Your Choice: Will you achieve and maintain Peak Performance State?

Lesson #6: Bias for Action

In athletics, the clock is ticking. In the workplace, time is money. In your family, quality time is priceless.

Author and leadership guru John Maxwell shares a story in his speaking appearances about when he was asked an important question by his father, who framed the question like this:

> *"Five frogs were sitting on a log and 4 decide to jump in. How many frogs are sitting on the log?"*

If you are like most reasonably intelligent people, you answered "one" — and you're wrong! There are still 5 frogs on that log because *deciding is different than doing!*

Too many people decide to be a better football player, better hoopster, better volleyball player, better gymnast, better hockey player, better student, better worker, better spouse or parent, but don't do what they need to do right now to move that decision or desire from simply being an intention to becoming a reality.

Before I get too far on this lesson, I must be very clear by what I mean when I say "bias" for action. Bias in this context is to *favor or prefer action over inaction.* It is a frame of mind, an attitude, that addresses an issue that I've observed in young people playing sports as well as professionals in the workplace at all ages, and in marriages and families. This frame of mind, once achieved, will help you recognize and efficiently manage the hundreds of decisions you face every day that will either move you toward your goals and desires, will get you stuck where you are, or will move you further away from where you want to go and where you want to be.

The Waiting Place

As I was finishing graduate school, I received a gift from the President of Northern Michigan University, Dr. James B. Appleberry, and his wonderful wife Pat, who had given me an opportunity and mentoring to grow in the world outside of athletics during my time in college. Their graduation and farewell gift to me included the classic book by Dr. Seuss entitled, *Oh, the Places You'll Go!* My favorite part of the book fits this lesson well and is a warning about the times when you are unclear about your next steps, the times when things just aren't going as you might have hoped, the times when you are questioning what is best. So in the way that only Dr. Seuss can say it, the warning goes:

> *You can get so confused*
> *that you'll start in to race*
> *down long wiggled roads at a break-necking pace*
> *and grind on for miles cross weirdish wild space,*
> *headed, I fear, toward a most useless place.*
> *The Waiting Place...*

> *...for people just waiting.*
> *Waiting for a train to go*
> *or a bus to come, or a plane to go*
> *or the mail to come, or the rain to go*
> *or the phone to ring, or the snow to snow*
> *or the waiting around for a Yes or No*

or waiting for their hair to grow.
Everyone is just waiting.

Waiting for the fish to bite
or waiting for the wind to fly a kite
or waiting around for Friday night
or waiting, perhaps, for their Uncle Jake
or a pot to boil, or a Better Break
or a string of pearls, or a pair of pants
or a wig with curls, or Another Chance.
Everyone is just waiting.

NO!
That's not for you!

Somehow you'll escape
all that waiting and staying
You'll find the bright places
where Boom Bands are playing.

With banner flip-flapping,
once more you'll ride high!
Ready for anything under the sky.
Ready because you're that kind of a guy!

And that kind of guy or gal is one who has developed a *Bias for Action.*

80-20 Rule

You may have heard of the "80-20 rule," which is a rule-of-thumb for making decisions. The theory of the 80-20 rule is that you can make a wise and timely decision with about 80%

of the information, rather than spending the extra time and effort it would take to get more information. Usually, the effort and time it takes to get the remaining 20% of the information means too much delay, often missing the critical timing for a decision, and in the end would not have impacted the final decision anyway. To delay a decision is quite often the same as making the decision to do nothing — which is commonly the wrong decision. Again, this is simply a rule-of-thumb or a mental model to help people make decisions in a timely manner. You can drive yourself crazy trying to specifically measure 80% of the information needed to make a decision. However, it's a good way to check yourself or others faced with making a decision. Are we about 80-20 with knowing what we need to know about this topic to make a good decision? If so, then decide and move to action.

Analysis Paralysis

You may have also heard of the phrase "analysis paralysis," which is the condition of prolonging the analysis of information being used to make a decision to the point of never really getting to the point of making the decision — often missing the critical deadline or window of opportunity for the decision to be made. At times, the fear of making a wrong decision drives leaders to fall victim to analysis paralysis until the time passes to make a good decision. Again, this concept is not to be taken literally; there is no paralysis involved here, but instead a term that can be used when you are noticing a lot of activity, discussion, debate, but it is not moving the decision-makers any closer to actually making a decision. Are we suffering from analysis paralysis on this topic? Can we make a decision with what we know today? If we cannot decide now, what do we truly need in order to make that decision and what is our final deadline?

Most Decisions Aren't Life or Death — Some Are

In my experience with leaders faced with big decisions in the workplace, the vast majority of those decisions can be made with about 80% of the information and can be made immediately when about 80% of the information is presented or otherwise made available. Usually, multiple good alternatives exist to address a problem or to take advantage of a business opportunity, without one "right" alternative. But too often those who do not have a bias for action fail to decide on one of the good alternatives, wishing for a more perfect solution. And in doing so, they often miss the ideal timing to act, and worse, proceed to waste more valuable time, energy, money, and other limited resources by waiting or by continuing to analyze alternatives.

Certainly, some decisions may require more information than the 80-20 rule. Some may in fact need to be "right" instead of simply a good alternative. Certain "life and death" decisions may be worth the added time and energy to find the remaining 10-20% of information or data, and will not be hurt by a delay in timing. For example, getting a second, third, or fourth doctor's opinion on a major elective surgery may be prudent, but if the patient is near death and worsening quickly, it clearly is not the prudent path. Even in cases of life and death, such as tactical decisions during a war, can easily result in more death simply by delaying the decision to act.

Finally, some decisions require a group consensus, unanimous agreement, a majority vote, or some other legal or administrative procedural requirement before a decision can be made. If any of these reasons clearly require a delay, then the key decision makers must push hard to take only the time truly required for further analysis or to satisfy the procedural requirements. But they must do so as efficiently and quickly and possible; their bias for action can help make the process as fast and efficient as possible.

Bias for Action in Athletics

Gametime!

In a game situation, quarterbacks, in a couple short seconds, must read the defense, make a decision, and take action — either throw it to a spot, directly to a receiver, run, or throw it out of bounds. Waiting even one second too long can get the quarterback sacked or force a pass too late. Linebackers must immediately read the movement of the offensive linemen and fill a hole or drop back in pass coverage. They must decide which person to cover or hit almost immediately. Waiting means bigger holes, open receivers, and more yardage the wrong way.

Gymnasts know their routine and rhythm; they must go for the next move on cue, disregarding all doubt, soreness, pressure, or any other distraction. They have prepared themselves for their moment and know when it is time to 'go for it' almost without thinking.

The speed of a hockey game doesn't allow for even seconds of thinking or waiting. The preparation and mindset of hockey players result in lightning fast game action with players reacting out of habit and split second creativity and decision-making. The fast pace of a hockey game results in many turnovers and missed passes and shots, but there is no other alternative to hold the puck and wait.

In the heat of an athletic game or performance, those who wait will fail.

Bias for Action in Athletic Preparation

Even way before the actual game or performance, athletes are constantly faced with decisions that will move them more toward their goals or further away from their goals. Do I workout now or later? Which workout should I do today? What shots should I work on today? Do I need to study my playbook? Should I go over my routine again? If so, when is the best time?

Those athletes who have a bias for action will, for example, get their workouts done as soon as they can, often making it the first priority of the day. They will be the first to agree to meet a teammate to play catch, run, or lift. They are the first to try a new workout that might give them better results. They can create effective workouts even when their gym is closed - pushups, pull-ups, lunges, sprints, stretching, etc. know no schedules and need no gym — they find a way. They reach out to coaches for feedback and advice. They are constantly looking for better ways to train and take action to improve their training. They avoid ruts.

Failed athletes are often waiting athletes. They wait for the coach to send a training schedule. They wait for the gym to open. They wait for better weather. They wait for their favorite workout partner. They wait for tomorrow instead of acting today. They wait for coaches to tell them what to do. They wait for a better coach. They wait for colleges to recruit them. As a result, they will wait for their opportunity to play, to start, and to be the best they can be.

Let's Get Better, Let's Go

Steve Young is one of the most successful quarterbacks of all times, including multiple NFL MVP and Super Bowl MVP honors, 6 passing titles, and several records at the time of his retirement. One of his many successful traits was that he had a Bias for Action. For example, as told to me by his coach at the time, Steve Mariucci, the two Steves (Steve Young and Coach "Mooch" as they call him) were in an offseason meeting to talk about "red zone" plays. These are plays designed to score from close to end zone (20 yard line and closer). Young was 37 years old at the time, which is getting old for an NFL athlete, and he had already achieved most of his success as an NFL star. So after the two had reviewed the red zone plays in great detail in the meeting room, the "old" highly successful veteran quarterback said, "Let's get better, let's go!" He insisted on immediately going out to the practice field with his coach and a few other players to practice the red zone throws, to begin mentally and physically honing and mastering the plays and the throws. He not only was coachable (Lesson #1: Be Coachable), he was demanding in the way he learned and then took action immediately to get better.

Steve Young certainly could have taken the stance that since it was the offseason there would be plenty of time to test out these plays later. There was more than enough time to practice before the start of the next season. But with a Bias for Action, Steve Young was able to begin the process of improving that day, which then enabled even more time to hone the plays and become even more expert in making the throws. But becoming a Hall of Fame quarterback doesn't happen by saying, "I'll do it later."

Bias for Action in the Workplace

The same dynamic applies in the workplace. I have found it almost always better for an individual or a team to take the action that they believed to be right based on a sufficient amount of information and acceptable conditions rather than waiting or searching for more information, waiting for ideal conditions, or waiting for somebody else to tell them what to do.

A popular old saying that fits this lesson, especially in the workplace, is:

"It's better to get forgiveness than permission."

That quote has become a rallying slogan or core value in many newer companies and by some of the most recognized successful entrepreneurs. There are several variations of this quote, but all drive the same message. If you want to succeed in life, then don't wait for anybody to tell you what you know you need to do to succeed. This doesn't mean to do anything illegal or otherwise inappropriate, but it does challenge those you, especially those working in companies with multiple levels of management and/or a culture that slows down innovation, to take risks and do what you believe is the best way to achieve success.

Amazing Grace

To make the quote even more powerful, look at who is credited with first saying it or at least is known as the person who first made the quote popular. Not too many people have heard of Dr. Grace Harper, also known as "Amazing Grace," who was born way back in 1906. She earned a PhD from Yale University and worked on the U.S. military's protocomputer project at Harvard, the Harvard Mark I, during World War II. She also developed the first computer compiler. Later, Dr. Harper became one of the first women to be promoted to rear admiral in the U.S. Navy.

Her state of mind, a bias for action, enabled her to focus on what she knew needed to be done to succeed and not get distracted by the many hurdles that could have diverted her, including the fact that not too many women earned PhDs from Ivy League schools at that time, hardly any women were in the military, even fewer were in leadership roles in the military, mathematicians were almost all men, and almost nobody had ever even seen a computer in the 1940s. [21]

---

[21] Bill Murphy Jr., Inc. Magazine, Jan. 20, 2016, "Want to Succeed in Life? Ask for Forgiveness, Not Permission". Also Encyclopedia Brittanica

The Sad Cycle of Inaction

I recall many times over my career when a team was scheduled to present research and make a recommendation to a senior leader or to a senior leadership team. And an unfortunate phenomenon would often occur; I'm calling this the 'sad cycle of inaction.'

The signature phase of the sad cycle of inaction, which occurs immediately following the presentation and recommendation by the team, became known as the question pump. The leader or leaders would ask many questions of the presenting team. Some leaders would ask rhetorical questions (questions asked not really to get an answer but to make a point to the presenters or to the other meeting attendees). Other leaders would ask questions to demonstrate that they were well-versed on the subject matter and did their best to catch the presenters on a mistake, a typo, a math error - the gotcha questions. Still others would ask questions to ensure that their peers were hearing their opinion. But certainly others would ask helpful questions in a sincere attempt to clarify the work and proposal being presented — these questions were in fact adding value and making progress toward a decision, action, progress.

Now let me back up a little, back to before the presentation. Knowing that the question pump had a high probability to occur, the presenting team would normally have done its best to prepare fully for any and all questions that may come up from the leaders in the presentation, including preparing for questions that aren't necessarily relevant to the decision, but that somebody *may* ask based on their particular role and/or unique interests. This often translated to hours of added preparation, including involving more people in the research, more homework for team members, and the normally unpopular *pre-meetings* — and, at times, dreaded *pre-meetings to the pre-meetings*. At some point, time would run out on the team; they would normally scramble up until the last minute, regardless how well prepared they really were, changing slides and other documents in an attempt to answer as many questions as could come up in the presentation.

Now back to the presentation. In response to the questions asked by the senior leaders, the presenting team would normally answer the vast majority of the questions. And almost always, there was enough information for the leadership in that moment to either make a decision to:

1. Approve the recommendation

2. Approve the recommendation with suggested changes, or

3. Reject the recommendation

However, given that there were normally a few questions that weren't answered completely by the presenting team, or weren't answered to the satisfaction of a particular questioner, the cycle of inaction would often continue to the next phase. The team would be sent back to do more homework and to answer the questions that weren't answered, including a debrief meeting, more research, and more meetings to check on status of answers to the remaining questions. Meanwhile, they would work to reschedule a follow-up presentation (which could be weeks later). When rescheduled, the presenting team would often have to re-present the research and proposal as a reminder for the leadership team (since weeks had passed since the last presentation) and, commonly, for meeting attendee(s) who weren't able to be at the last presentation. The presenting team then provides answers to the questions left unanswered in the last meeting. Some new questions could be asked. The presenting team would do its best to answer the new questions, then hope and pray that the cycle would not repeat itself for another follow-up. And so on. This is not unusual in the workplace.

The crazy part about the 'sad cycle of inaction' is that most of the questions that slowed down the entire process often didn't impact the decision to be made with any meaningful significance. The time and energy wasted throughout this phenomenon are in fact a part of the final decision, adding costs, lowering the morale of the team, missing opportunities during the delay by distracting the team, and so on. When, on the other hand, a leader or a team has a "bias for action," they are able to take sufficient information (despite not having all information) and make educated decisions efficiently.

I'll have to admit, I have been a key player in the cycle of action over my career, in every role that I described in the scenario above. I've been in the frustrating position of making the presentations and not getting resolution for weeks or months. I've also been responsible for scheduling pre-meetings to pre-meetings to ensure that our presentation would go perfectly - thus wasting time and energy of my team. I've been the senior leader and on the senior leadership team as well, asking both good questions and wasteful questions, those questions that in hindsight didn't really make a significant difference on the decision that needed to be made. Especially later in my career, when I was in positions of higher leadership, I did my best to point out when the cycle of inaction was grinding us down as an organization and pushed my fellow colleagues to have a bias for action.

I'll leave the sad cycle of inaction example with a reminder to leaders of organizations — and a warning to you for when you are in leadership positions. For the most part, as a leader, you don't make much of anything. You don't make products, you don't make the services that make your customers happy, you don't make components, you really don't make much for your company or organization — *but you should be making big decisions*. And if you are in fact making big decisions, you are playing your position and making a big impact on your organization. If you are not making big decisions, then you are probably making mostly noise and more work for your teams. This reminder is one that the Ford North America Business Unit President, Kumar Galhotra, used to explicitly remind and review with his leadership team every Friday. At the end of each week, we would go over every key decision made that week and then look forward to the big decisions that would likely need to be made the following week. If the page of decisions was sparse, it was a challenge to the leadership to consider what needed to be decided in order to enable the broader team to execute the plan. The larger team of tens of thousands of employees were probably waiting on some decision by their leaders. These key decisions certainly include decisions not to take a particular action. Deciding to cut a major program, for example, is infinitely better than prolonging the work by the team on a dying program. A bias-for-action mindset includes making decisions to stop doing work that is not deemed as essential to achieving the teams goals. In other words, a "no" decision is good, but "no decision" is bad.

Don't Worry About Worrying, Execute the Plan

I've referenced earlier in this book, one of the best leaders with whom I had the privilege of working while he was the CEO of Ford Motor Company, Alan Mulally. In my first meeting with him in person, back in 2006, one of the other meeting participants asked him what kept him up at night. His answer was, "Nothing really. I sleep well." But wait! The company was expected to lose about $14 billion that year and likely fall into bankruptcy; how could he not worry?! But as everybody in the room was stunned by his answer and thinking the same crazy thoughts, he went on to explain that he doesn't "worry about worrying." He shared that he was confident in his team, he was confident in the plan they put together, and his focus was on delivering the plan. Like Grace Harper, mentioned above, he didn't allow distractions to take his focus off of what he knew had to be done now to succeed later. And through the hard work of the entire Ford team, with a focus on the actions in the plan, we were able to come out of one of the greatest recessions in the history of the U.S. and global economies, without taking any government bailout money, and went on to deliver years of record and near-record profits with better products and higher employee morale.

Get Out of the Huddle

In Lesson #3, I mentioned Todd Penegor, my high school friend and teammate in basketball and football and presently the CEO of Wendy's. Todd shared with me his message to his global leadership team in the heat of the COVID-19 pandemic and consistent with Lesson #6: Bias for Action. He also shared this message with his entire workforce. He told them:

> *"We are the leaders that we have been waiting for…no one else is going to get it done for us. For all of you, now is your time. Take advantage of the opportunity to show everyone what you are capable of doing. Have the courage to make the call, then focus on great execution. Don't spend forever in the huddle trying to figure out which play to run. Start marching the ball down the field. You may get called for a few penalties along the way or get sacked a few times, but keep going. It is the only way you are going to score."*

Bias for Action in light of COVID-19

As a recent example, in the midst of the coronavirus pandemic, I listened to a message from Dr. Michael Ryan, the World Health Organization Executive Director, who spoke of the critical importance of acting quickly when battling a virus spread. He said,

> *"You need to act quickly…be fast…have no regrets…you must be the first mover…If you need to be right before you move, you will never win..Perfection is the enemy of the good. Speed trumps*

perfection. The problem in society that we have at the moment is everyone is afraid of making a mistake. Everyone is afraid of the consequences of error. But the greatest error is not to move. The greatest error is to be paralyzed by the fear of failure."

I recognize that the World Health Organization and its leaders were questioned and criticized during the pandemic, and rightfully so in certain respects, but the message by Dr. Ryan in this instance stands on its own merits and is exactly what I'm talking about in this lesson.

Career Planning

A common scenario that I quite frequently addressed over my career working in human resources was counseling employees about their career decisions. Early in their careers, recent high school and college graduates are wondering and planning what they should do for a living. Most really don't have a clue what they will end up doing longterm for a career, and that is both perfectly normal and OK. Some had a very good idea about what they wanted to pursue and even among that group, preferences often changed once they got a taste for what they thought they wanted. Very few pick one path early in their careers and stick with it throughout their working life. In a 2019 study by the Bureau of Labor Statistics, the average professional changed jobs more than 12 times over a career. As it relates to this lesson, my advice to those feeling stuck with deciding on their long-term career, is to set a short timeline (days not weeks) to lay out all of the decision criteria that you value. Then lay out the best options you have ahead of you for the next step on your journey, then make a decision as to the step you will take. There is almost never a clear right and wrong — every option has pros and cons, pluses and minuses. Avoid getting stuck in a high anxiety or depressed state of mind worrying about what you should be doing about your career. As you work hard in your current job or situation, study your alternatives, decide what is best to do now, and work/act to make that decision a good decision. If that doesn't work, then take another shot. Beware of sitting in a position, unhappy, unfulfilled, with no plan in place to improve your situation — act now toward getting out of that career trap. Some will say, "Oh that sounds so easy" as a crutch to remain in their state of misery without taking action. So I'll reply with another challenge, "Why can't it be easy?"

On numerous occasions, I counseled employees who were not happy in their jobs or in their careers. And in several of those situations, after months or years of dissatisfaction, these same people were let go from the company (call it laid off, fired, terminated, or other term) as a result of corporate downsizing or restructuring. And at first, in just about every case, the person was devastated. Even though they were not happy with their job, losing it was a completely different level of concern and fear of the future. Each went through their own version of grief, feeling shock and anger, then rationalizing what had happened to them. After a few days, weeks, or months, in just about every case, the person found a new job that gave them more responsibility and flexibility in their working schedule which enabled a better work-life balance; and about half of them found higher pay on top of all that. Despite being unhappy for months or years, it took somebody else to force them to get out of a bad situation, which then ended up being better overall. If they had more of a bias for action in this regard, they could have reduced the time spent being unhappy, saved the trauma of being fired, could have eliminated or reduced the time it took to search and find a new job, and could have lessened the pain of not knowing what the future would hold for a new job and financial security.

Certainly, there are cases where somebody doesn't find a better job and ends up in a worse situation. But in my experience, this was the exception and not the rule.

Bias for Action in the Family

Greatness Around the House

If you want to become a star around your house during your school years and then when visiting home on vacation breaks, walk in the door with a bias-for-action and watch your parents light up. When you see dishes in the sink, quickly clean them or put them in the dishwasher. If your room is a mess, take a couple minutes and simply make the bed and straighten it up (even piling in the closet is better than the appearance of chaos). If it's garbage day, take a minute or two and bring the cans to the street.

The College Decision

A timely example that some of you young student-athletes may have already experienced or are about to experience very soon — the decision of whether to go to college and, for most of you, which college to attend. I'm not going to minimize the importance of doing your research and taking the time to actually visit those colleges that you have identified as high on your list. But I will in fact challenge you and your parents and coaches to have a bias for action in how you identify your top choices and then in how you make a final decision. Especially during the phase when my sons where searching for colleges, I spoke with dozens of parents and prospective college students about their process and, most notably, their state of mind. I was blown away with how stressful many (probably most) people allowed that process to be.

In my experience, the college search was one of the most enjoyable times I had with my sons.

They were typical students and pretty good athletes, both of which were interested in being student-athletes in college. They were not highly recruited in their respective sports, but had interest from multiple teams, and their grades were decent, but were not going to get them into the top academic schools. But regardless of whether you are highly recruited, partially recruited, or not being recruited at all, having a bias-for-action mindset will enable you to lay out your plan, work your plan by taking the steps you know are necessary to succeed, and do not "worry about worrying." Enjoy this special journey. It is not only possible, it is a shame for anybody to miss out on the opportunity.

And if after several months, you look back at your college choice and don't believe it was the right choice, then heed this exact same lesson, develop a new plan, take the actions that you know are needed to either succeed where you are or in selecting what might be a better alternative. You did not make a mistake in selecting your first college. You perhaps learned what does not work for you and you will use those learnings to make the next decisions and execute your next plan - whether that is another college, a skilled trade, or another good option for that moment in your life.

Thought Leaders and Role Models on Bias for Action

"I learned a long time ago that there is something worse than missing the goal, and that's not pulling the trigger."

— Mia Hamm,
Olympic Champion multiple times and one of world's best women soccer players of all time.

"Some people want it to happen, some wish it would happen, others make it happen."

— Michael Jordan,
arguably the greatest basketball player of all time.

"I'd rather regret the risks that didn't work out than the chances I didn't take at all."

— Simone Biles,
Olympic Gold medalist

"Greatness doesn't wait."

– Mitch Hancock,
former All American Wrestler and now coach of Detroit
Catholic Central Wrestling, one of the top high school
wrestling programs in the U.S.

*"Cautious, careful people, always casting about to preserve their
reputations can never effect a reform."*

— Susan B. Anthony,
American social reformer and women's rights activist who
played a pivotal role in the women's suffrage movement.

*"I didn't get there by wishing for it or hoping for it,
but by working for it."*

— Estée Lauder,
an American businesswoman and founder of the Estée
Lauder Companies, a pioneering cosmetics company. She was
also one of the wealthiest self-made women entrepreneurs in
America.

*"The most difficult thing is the decision to act,
the rest is merely tenacity."*

— Amelia Earhart,
aviation pioneer and author and the first female aviator to fly
solo across the Atlantic Ocean.

"I'd rather regret the things I've done than regret the things I haven't done."

— Lucille Ball,
actress, comedienne, model, entertainment studio executive and producer.

"You miss 100% of the shots you don't take."

— Wayne Gretzky,
"The Great One" who is considered the greatest hockey player ever by many sportswriters, players, and the NHL itself.

"Do. Or do not. There is no try."

— Yoda,
from the movie The Empire Strikes Back

"The best time to plant a tree was 20 years ago. The second best time is now."

— popular Chinese proverb made famous in my extended family by a great man and mentor, the late **R. Scott Custer**

And finally, a classic timeless quote from **Theodore Roosevelt**, 26th president of the United States:

"It is not the critic who counts; not the man who points out how the strong man stumbles, or where the doer of deeds could have done them better. The credit belongs to the man who is actually in the arena, whose face is marred by dust and sweat and blood; who strives valiantly; who errs, who comes short again and again,

because there is no effort without error and shortcoming; but who does actually strive to do the deeds; who knows great enthusiasms, the great devotions; who spends himself in a worthy cause; who at the best knows in the end the triumph of high achievement, and who at the worst, if he fails, at least fails while daring greatly, so that his place shall never be with those cold and timid souls who neither know victory nor defeat."

Your Choice: Will you have a Bias for Action?

Lesson #7: Discipline as a Habit

A simple working definition of discipline:

> **Doing what you *know* you should do, *when* you should do it, whether you *like it or not*.**

This lesson is dependent on the clarity of Lesson #3 - Play Your Position(s) Well. Because only if you are clear on the expectations of you in the positions you play — in athletics, at work, and in your family — can you then know what you should do and when you should do it.

Once you are clear on your primary positions and jobs you play in your life, then you can begin forming the habit of discipline around what it will take to prepare for and to achieve the desired results in those positions.

This lesson is also dependent on being successful in Lesson #6 - Bias for Action. Most people will immediately agree that being disciplined around things like a healthy diet, getting sufficient sleep, and exercising regularly will only help somebody lead a longer and healthier life than if they didn't exercise, smoked, and didn't get enough sleep. However, as described in Lesson #6 - Bias for Action, there is a difference between *deciding* to be healthy and taking the *actions* to be healthy. When discipline is not yet a habit, moving from deciding to acting is often drudgery, painful, and just not fun.

As with any habit, when discipline becomes a habit, it becomes natural and almost effortless to live the way you know you should live and want to live. When discipline becomes a habit, you almost don't think about what you should do and when and how you should do it, you just know it subconsciously — and you find yourself in fact doing what you know you should do, when you should do it. The question of whether you like it or not becomes less and less relevant as the habit becomes more engrained in your character. It becomes the way you are, the way you roll.

As discipline becomes a habit, you naturally identify what you know you should do, when you should do it, and then you follow-through without evaluating whether you liked it or not. And on the rare occasion that you don't follow-through with the intended action, that now generates the feeling that something wasn't right, even a feeling of disappointment. Think about it. Before you developed the habit of working out hard every day, it took effort to get ready to workout, get to the gym, and then to workout hard. It maybe even made you grumpy to go through the entire process. But after you develop the habit of the daily hard workout, the grumpiness is essentially gone and the workout happens without the mental effort needed to self-motivate. As a matter of fact, the grumpiness generally comes back on the days that you miss a workout. Your "disciplined self" just knows when you did not do what you knew you should have done on that day. When discipline is a habit, you feel it physically and mentally when you fall off the path that you've established for your success.

Discipline As a Habit in Athletics

In athletics, discipline can be noticed in the smallest details. When a team is running sprints, do you notice every single player putting their hand on the starting line — not behind the line, not in front of the line, but on the line? Is every player running the drill properly, without looking to see if a coach is watching, and then sprinting through the finish line on every drill and every practice? In a game, discipline shows up in the number of penalties, assignments missed, receivers left uncovered, tackles missed, turnovers, and mental mistakes.

In almost all cases, your coaches sincerely care about you and about the success of your team. So when they are pushing you to do what you and they *know* you should do, *when* you should do it, and they know you don't like it, they are helping you be the best version of yourself; they are helping your team be the best team it can be.

Discipline as a "Form of Love"

Hall of Fame coach Tom Izzo of the Michigan State University Spartans calls discipline a "form of love." He said he learned that from coach Buck Nystrom who was my coach at Northern Michigan University and who pushed me to be a better quarterback. As you watch coach Izzo or coach Nystrom on the sidelines, they are not holding back at all when they get in the faces of their players - literally. And yet, in the end, when the games, seasons, and careers are over, their players love them. They may not love their coach at the moment of getting yelled at, and they may legitimately have a complaint about some aspect of their coaching, but they recognize at some point that their coach wanted the absolute best for them and was doing their best to make them the best they could be by insisting on excellence. I know both Coach Izzo and Coach Buck well enough to know that they truly love their players and the process of making their players better athletes and better people. They would do anything they could to help their players become the best they can be, especially off the basketball court or football field.

Poor discipline in athletics, through time, normally results in unprepared teams, losing games, losing seasons, "off the field" problems, and unrealized potential.

Discipline As a Habit in the Workplace

In the workplace, quality products and services are the result of disciplined workers consistently following production processes and service protocols, meeting customer expectations, on time and within budget. Workplace discipline can be seen in companies that go beyond the basics of following the law (i.e. paying taxes, complying with regulatory standards), but go further and follow-through on what they say they are all about; in other words, they live up to their brand promises with their actions. Workplace discipline can be also be observed in how the most basic procedures are followed. For example, disciplined Electricians always follow safety procedures, especially critical procedures like properly shutting off high voltage power before working on machines.

The consequence of poor discipline in the workplace is waste in many forms — wasted time, wasted money, wasted equipment, wasted skills, wasted effort — all of which reduce the competitiveness of the company, with lower profits and less ability to reinvest in the business and in the people on the team. In the example of the Electrician or other dangerous professions following safety procedures, poor discipline results in the loss of life or other serious injuries. Over 3,500 people died in the workplace in the US in 2019 [22], many of which could have been prevented if somebody (either management, co-workers, or the person who died in the accident) did what they knew they should have done, when they should have done it, whether they liked it or not.

In my career, I had the chance to work in multiple manufacturing facilities, was responsible for human resources in several of them, and visited still others. It was quite obvious after getting familiar with these plants to recognize that the workplaces with a culture of discipline had the highest quality, lowest cost, and best safety performance. And as a bonus, they normally had the highest employee morale. What might begin as painful for employees to follow strict work rules and safety precautions later results in higher team performance and higher morale.

Seeing Discipline at Work

In the workplace, discipline can be noticed by the cleanliness of the office, the showroom, the plant, the kitchen, and especially the restrooms. Important procedures and policies are effectively communicated, usually posted clearly in the open, and followed. To-do lists, project management software,

---

[22] https://www.osha.gov/fatalities

or other tools are used to track the progress of assignments through to actual completion.

The behaviors of workers in a disciplined workplace result in meetings starting on time and ending on time (or ending early), responding to customers and each other in a timely manner (emails, phone calls, texts messages), high attendance, hardly anybody "calls in sick" (which is different than actually being sick). Distractions to the core work to be done is minimized.

When discipline is a habit for a team in the workplace, the compliance to rules and procedures is not driven by fear, such as fear of being fired or fear of the boss, but is driven instead by the clarity of the purpose and then the habit itself. You see, long ago the team bought into the idea that discipline in core work practices would enable the best results for the team, which inspired them to work toward forming the habit of discipline in the workplace, which then became the driving force of compliance to the critical procedures and work rules. And in time, the right behaviors became the right habits which then produce the right results.

Discipline As a Habit in the Family

Often, the word *discipline* in the context of the family is associated with getting in trouble, having consequences for "being bad", timeouts, spanking, and so on. Not here. In this context, discipline holds the same definition, just now in the family setting:

> **Doing what you *know* you should do, *when* you should do it, whether you *like it or not*.**

As with sports or a job, having family discipline begins with knowing what you're trying to accomplish. Common goals of families often include loving, supporting, helping, and protecting each family member to help them be the best person they can be.

In your family, discipline can be seen when every family member is pitching in to help out around the house, picking up after themselves, taking responsibility for doing chores without being reminded over and over, manners at the table, avoidance of emotional hurtful outbursts between family members, and family members holding themselves accountable for upholding their family values. When doing the right things around the house feels like 'hard work' and is met with heavy sighs and groans, the family isn't quite there yet. These sighs and groans are seeds that if not stopped will blossom into a lack of discipline. You get what you tolerate. Lack of discipline in a family can easily pull a family apart. But when each family member is able to do what they know they should be doing for the family, when they should be doing it, whether they like it or not, the entire family wins.

Pick a Chore to Be Your Home Discipline Habit

One way to practice Discipline as a Habit, as well as Play Your Position Well (Lesson #3), at home, is to pick a chore or two and develop that into your signature home habit(s). I did this with the simple task of washing dishes. In my family, my sons and my wife enjoy cooking; they especially enjoy it with each other when they are home from college or during a holiday from work. They like trying new dishes, experimenting with seasonings, and making new creations out of what is in the fridge and on the shelves. They even enjoy watching the Food Channel! I, on the other hand, have zero interest in cooking, maybe less than zero, and would rather dig ditches in a rainstorm than prepare a big dinner. But I love to eat their creations. So I figured maybe being the "dishes dude" could be a good home habit for me to own. It is needed. I have the capability, being the highly skilled dishwasher that I've become. And since it encourages good meals, gives the cooks peace of mind that they don't need to later clean up, and keeps the house tidy, it is well worth the little effort and time it takes me. In your family, look for the chore or two that you can develop as your home habit(s).

Habit of Supporting Family Members

My niece Emily, who developed a strength as being 100% supportive of her team and teammates in highly competitive high school and club volleyball and then later as a D1 collegiate MVP, suggests picking that attribute as another home habit — the attribute of being supportive of your family members. For example, going to your brother's hockey games, sitting in the cold at your sister's band performance at halftime, showing interest in what your parents or siblings find interesting (even when it isn't that interesting!), listening to each other's stories at the dinner table, acknowledging what others are saying or feeling before you shift the story to you and what you want to say and feel, are all ways to be supportive of your family members. Emily found that once you reach the habit stage on this one, you find yourself truly getting more interested in and caring for what matters to your family members and as a result growing in love and unity as a family. This is not to say that you have to agree with everything in your family, but even your disagreements can be handled in a way that honors the others' points of view.

Forming a Habit

So how does somebody form a habit? How long can it take for a behavior to become a habit? Well, there is no easy answer to this, but I can offer some insights. Based on recent research, it can take anywhere from 18 to 254 days for a person to form a new habit and an average of 66 days for a new behavior to become automatic.[23]

So it really depends on several factors including the habit being formed, the motivation of the individual, the frequency of attempting the desired behavior, and so on. In the broad sense of discipline as a habit though, once a person makes the connection between discipline and getting the desired results (in athletics, at work, or in the family), this can kick in relatively quickly on the timeline of habits. Because every day, you are faced with up to hundreds of decisions as you go about your day, even as you sit and relax. Once your priority goals are clear (see Lesson #2 Doing Your Job Well), your habit of discipline will entail a constant consideration of the fundamental questions:

What should I be doing now to do my job(s) well? — do that now (Lesson #6 Bias for Action)

---

[23] https://www.healthline.com/health/how-long-does-it-take-to-form-a-habit#takeaway

What else should I be doing later and when? — plan it, schedule it, then do it on schedule

Note: Rest and sleep are an important part of discipline. Answering the questions above does not suggest going full throttle at all times. Rest is an action. Relaxation is required to be successful over the long haul. You must be disciplined to not overwork yourself, just as importantly as to not underwork yourself.

An Important Judge

One of my favorite poems from my days playing sports is called, *"The Man in the Glass."* Along with my college football summer workout binder, my coaches would include this poem inside the front cover. It's an old poem, as you can tell by some of the words and phrases, and there is question as to who even first wrote it. I've seen several versions. But this is the one I memorized in college, because in the end, discipline is about what you do when nobody else is looking. You know if you have done what you know you should have done, when you should have done it, whether you liked it or not.

Note: You young women can rest assured that the reference to 'man' in this poem equally applies to you as well.

The Man in the Glass

When you come out on top in your struggle for self
and the world makes you king for a day
Just go to the mirror and look at yourself
and see what that man has to say.

For it isn't your father or mother or wife
whose verdict upon you must pass
The person whose verdict counts most in your life
is the one staring back from the glass.

Some people may think you a straight-shooting chum
and call you a heck-of-a guy
But the man in the glass says you're only a bum
if you can't look him straight in the eye.

He's the fellow to please never mind all the rest
for he's with you clear up to the end
And you've passed your most dangerous difficult test
if the man in the glass is your friend.

You may fool the whole world down the pathway
of life and get pats on the back as you pass
But your final reward will be heartaches and
tears if you've cheated the man in the glass.

Thought Leaders and Role Models for Discipline as a Habit

"Set realistic goals, keep re-evaluating, and be consistent."

– Venus Williams,
World top ranked tennis player on three different occasions
and winner of multiple Olympic gold medals

"It doesn't matter what you're trying to accomplish. It's all a matter of discipline."

– Wilma Rudolph,
Olympic Champion who overcame childhood disabilities to compete in the 1956 Summer Olympic Games, and in 1960, she became the first American woman to win three gold medals in track and field at a single Olympics.

"Discipline is the bridge between goals and accomplishment."

— St. Teresa of Calcutta,
founder of the Order of the Missionaries of Charity, a Roman Catholic congregation of women dedicated to helping the poor. Considered one of the 20th Century's greatest humanitarians, she was canonized as Saint Teresa of Calcutta in 2016

"...and keep running until I forget about you!"

— Coach Buck Nystrom,
there is nobody else like him!

Final Word on Discipline as a Habit

For this lesson, Discipline as a Habit, I'll leave you with a simple but powerful 'starter kit,' whether in athletics, the workplace, or in your family. Begin building the habit of discipline with these three habits:

- *Be on time.* To be crystal clear, this means be early for everything. Actions may include putting every appointment and deadline in one calendar on your phone with start time or due date before the actual deadline.

- *Do what you say you'll do.* Actions may include a sound "to do" list or "commitment tracking."

- *Give 100% effort.* Never take a scheduled "workday" off, including scheduled practices, game day, work day at your job, or time with your family. Actions may include visual reminders of your goals, daily reflections on what you did well, and memorizing the essence of discipline: *Do what you know you should do, when you should do it, whether you like it or not.*

Your Choice: Will you make Discipline a Habit?

Lesson #8: Get the Best of Everyone

Several years ago, I had the privilege of meeting a young man in his mid-20s by the name of Xavier DeGroat. Xavier is the Founder and CEO of the Xavier DeGroat Autism Foundation (XDAF), an organization that is focused on creating and promoting opportunities for people with autism through advocacy, education, economic opportunities, and humanitarian efforts. Xavier founded this organization through his passion for those with autism, his determination, and his unique ability to make personal connections with just about anybody. His list and photos of friends and acquaintances include famous actors, senators, U.S. presidents, other world leaders, superstar athletes, religious leaders, top business leaders, and others. I serve on the board of his foundation. Xavier himself is autistic. He used to be bullied when he was growing up, especially in high school. Back then, Xavier didn't understand the concept of sarcasm and, as a result, could not recognize when his classmates and others were making fun of him. When Xavier would finally recognize the mean sarcasm, it was usually too late and after their cruelty led to his embarrassment and emotional distress. So at a young age, Xavier made it his passion to help those with autism by also helping those without autism to understand and to become better as a society in how it deals with those with autism.

When Xavier begins working with somebody new to advance the work of his foundation, or in developing new relationships with people he meets along his journey, he relishes the moment when that person says something like, "I don't think about your autism anymore, because I'm impressed with you." When Xavier hears that, he knows that he has shifted that person's perspective away from what might be viewed as an issue (having autism) to the skills and capabilities that a person possesses — in this case, Xavier's engaging personality, joy in meeting others, knowledge and ideas on autism, and a passion to make a difference through his foundation.

"Ability matters more than your disability," Xavier has told me on multiple occasions. He also has posted another one of his quotes on his website, "Autism isn't the problem. It's society."

With that appropriate introduction capturing the essence of Lesson #8 - Get the Best of Everybody, let's explore the mindset of Xavier and the concept of focusing on what people can do instead of what they can't do more deeply across athletics, career, and family.

Get the Best of Everyone in Athletics

I have always loved football especially among all the sports because it brings together a wide variety of unique characteristics (i.e. big, small, strong, less strong, fast, non-very-fast, rich, poor, black, white, brown, good grades, not-so-good grades, social, vocal, private, quiet, starters, non-starters, practice players, and so on). Football also comprises a variety of skills often unique to only a few positions (i.e. throwing, catching, blocking, tackling, kicking, punting, carrying the ball, and so on) and specific roles and responsibilities (i.e. offense, defense, special teams, linemen, running backs, linebackers, defensive backs, receivers, and so on), all coming together for a common cause and needing each other's different strengths, skills, and responsibilities to make a great team. A similar type of diversity is true for other sports in even more ways. My son's national champion collegiate soccer team, for example, comprised players from Britain, Scotland, France, and several states within the U.S., a global diversity not normally seen in American football.

But the most important part of a diverse team *is not their differences*. You read that correctly, the most import part of a diverse team *is not* their valuable and unique differences, though critically important those are, but the most important aspect for a team is *how each team member brings those differences together to make the team stronger*, to give the team a competitive advantage, to help the team be the best it can be, and to ultimately achieve their goals as a team.

Coaches in athletics are always attempting to match the skills they have on their team with the game-plan and plays that they are comfortable calling. The best coaches are able to maintain a certain level of consistency in their approach and style for continuity year over year, but also are able to make the adjustments necessary to take full advantage of the talent (or lack of talent) that they have on their team in any one season. The best coaches balance the need to treat each player fairly and consistently with respect to values and goals, but to deal with each individual player in a way that brings out the best in each of them. In doing so, their goal is to get the best out of each player in a way that will most benefit the team.

Team dynamics are crucial in athletics. Top talent and a good game-plan will still fail if the team dynamics are unhealthy — if players are arguing among themselves or with the coaches, when individuals have not already learned the other lessons and have not made the choices covered earlier in this book. When teammates and coaches appreciate what each player brings to the team and work to develop strengths instead of dwelling on the weaknesses of each player, then they are focused on getting the best of everyone, which will maximize the effectiveness of the team.

The Story of Airport

In my second year on the football team at Northern Michigan University, during the hot summer camp practices, I recall watching the short parade of the "uninvited walk-ons" come onto the field for their separate tryout. Those of us "on scholarship" as well as the "invited walk-ons" had already been at summer camp for a few days of practice and were living in the dorms as a team during this time. The NMU Wildcats were considered among the top in NCAA Division II football during that era. And as is done each year, a group of aspiring student athletes who were not normally recruited to play college football but had a desire to play were given a chance to tryout. This group almost never produced any players who made a significant impact on the team. This story sounds elitist and arrogant thus far, I know. But I'm simply describing how it was and not demeaning anybody. Most in this annual group of unknowns would tryout that day and never return. Some would stay for a few days or even weeks. Fewer yet might last a season, maybe two, but would rarely see action on the field during a game. It's just not how recruiting normally works for many of the college sports. The uninvited walk-on path is not an easy route and generally doesn't produce talent, especially for a top team. But then, every once in a while, there is an "Airport."

In that particular year, one of the unknowns taking the long-shot at making the team was a small guy from a small high school in a small town in the remote west end of the remote upper peninsula of Michigan. He played several positions on his small high school and received some honors as an interior lineman, though he only weighed about 160 pounds, which was small even for a defensive back in college. My overuse of the word 'small' is intentional here, just like the chances for this young man. He tried out hard and stuck around for another day. The next day, he worked hard again at practice. He did all the drills properly. He gave 100% on every drill. He stuck around another day. He started practicing with the defensive backs. Still nobody knew his name. He was not yet issued a practice jersey or shorts from the team. Every day, he wore a ratty old t-shirt with holes in it that was an advertisement for some airport. One day, one of the upperclassmen needed to call out to him during practice and since he didn't know his name blurted out, "Airport, over here." A few good chuckles and a new name was given to this unknown defensive back who was starting to show the talent and tenacity that suggested he just might belong on this team.

Over the next few days, "Airport" got his practice uniform and officially became a member of the team. Over the next few months, his relentless energy and performance shifted the focus of his coaches and us teammates away from his lack of size, lack of speed, his less-decorated high school career, and the fact that he was a long-shot walk-on — in other words, the characteristics that convinced us he couldn't help the team — and shifted all of our focus to how he gave 100% at every practice, made others around him work as hard, his attention to detail on every drill, his knowledge of the game, his comprehension of the defense, his ability to cover receivers who were faster than him, his tenacity at every practice, and his toughness — the characteristics that we knew could help the team.

And over the next couple years, Airport ended up being a two-year starter as a defensive back on one of the top-ranked teams nationally. As a senior, he was awarded all-conference. Yes, we did eventually learn his real name along the journey to be Brad, but even Brad cherishes to this day being called Airport by his former teammates, the name that originally meant *nobody* and yet ended up representing the epitome of an athletic success story.

Tips to Get the Best of Everyone in Athletics

To get the best of everybody in athletics, consider the following:

- Respect everybody — the starter, the last sub, the rookie, the no-name, even the "weird kid" since we all have our own share of weird.

- Know yourself — strengths, weaknesses, reputation, goals, motivation, triggers, etc.

- Be inclusive and get to know your teammates; make every one of them feel a part of the team

- Focus on what you and each teammate bring to the team vs. what you/they don't bring to the team

- Help build an environment where people can be at their best

Get the Best of Everyone in the Workplace

In the workplace, we have experts in Finance, Marketing, Design, Engineering, Skilled Trades, Human Resources, Clerical, and other areas of functional expertise. We have people from different countries and cultures, different races, religious beliefs and practices, people of almost all ages, generations X, Y, Z, Boomers, Echo-Boomers, Traditionalists, different genders, sexual orientation, and various abilities and disabilities. Still further, we have private people, sociable butterflies, those who are detail oriented while others are big picture thinkers. We have highly empathetic people, some deeply emotional, and stone cold "just the facts" thinkers. We have those who prefer to "wing it" or "play it by ear" and others who prefer, even need, a clear plan. Some work best under the pressure of a deadline and wait until the last minute to turn in an assignment, while others work much better starting early and finishing well in advance of a deadline.

In the workplace, these differences, along with countless more, are known as *diversity*. We work in very diverse workplaces that continue to get more diverse every day. In light of this diversity, making sure that these differences are recognized and respected by the members of the team, and then maximized for the benefit of the team is the most powerful aspect of a concept known as *inclusion*.

As I mentioned above when talking about the various skills and people on a sports team, the value is not as much in the differences that are inherent on a team, those differences are a given. They are the cards you're dealt and often the cards you've chosen. People are different in an infinite number of ways. The ability for a team to *recognize, honor, and maximize those differences to get the best* of *everyone* is the essence of inclusion and a key element to a successful team. Being different requires no skill and effort, and at times we focus too much on simply being different. The real value and even magic occurs when very different people learn to tap into the diverse skills, abilities, styles, perspectives, and passion of each member of the group to help each other perform better as a team, which in turn enables each team member to perform better as individuals. Overly focusing on differences divides teams while focusing on applying those differences to achieve common goals unites.

"Diversity, or the state of being different, isn't the same as inclusion. One is a description of what is, while the other describes a style of interaction essential to effective teams and organizations."

— Bill Crawford, Psychologist[24]

---

[24] Source: Leading Differently

"A diverse mix of voices leads to better discussions, decisions, and outcomes for everyone."

— Sundar Pichai,
CEO of Google[25]

The Importance of "Belonging"

I recently spoke with former co-worker of mine, Lori, who has held several prominent positions in human resources in corporate America. Lori is now responsible for Diversity and Inclusion at a Fortune 15 company. I asked Lori about what is most important to consider with respect to Diversity and Inclusion in the workplace these days. She immediately answered with the concept of "belonging." She explained that the feeling of belonging is a basic human need and it includes having the confidence that somebody "has your back" and will do whatever they can do to help you when you need it. And with that feeling of belonging, you will endure hardships and challenges and give your best effort so not to let the team down.

Then Lori shared a story about when she was in middle school and was playing volleyball with her middle school team. It was a difficult time in Lori's life as her parents were going through a divorce, which was weighing heavily on Lori, as well as the normal challenges for a middle school girl. To make matters worse, her volleyball teammates were "just mean," as Lori described it, so she decided to quit playing volleyball. Soon after, one of her former teammates stopped

---

[25] Source: Quartz at Work

Lori and asked why she quit; she told Lori that she was a good player and they wished she would have remained on the team. But Lori recalls not feeling like she belonged on that team with that group of girls. If her team would have helped her feel like she belonged, that experience may have been just what Lori needed to get through some of the other challenges in her life at that time.

So even now in her senior position in a Fortune 15 company, Lori recalls that middle school experience and can relate that same experience to what she is seeing in the workplace today. The concept of belonging in order to Get the Best of Everyone; so simple and yet so powerful whether it is in middle school volleyball or in one of the largest companies in the world.

Tools to Get the Best of Everyone

In the workplace, many tools are used to help individuals and teams better understand each others differences. Throughout my career in human resources, I had the privilege of learning and using effective tools that would help individuals and teams identify the differences that they had among them, different strengths, preferences, styles, weaknesses, perspectives, goals, desires, and more. Because in order to get the best of everybody, it is important first to know as much as you can about each other, including how you and your teammates prefer to operate while at work. When you know how each other prefers to operate, then you can help accommodate your teammates while they are helping to accommodating you and your preferences. When we are able to use our preferred methods of work, we are generally at our best and feel most competent, natural, and energetic.

A popular tool I have used frequently in my work is the Myers-Briggs Type Indicator. This tool is based on a theory of personality, called psychological type, developed by Swiss psychiatrist, Carl G. Jung, and it involves a series of questions across four categories within which people have very different (opposing) natural preferences.

1. **Where do you focus your attention? Where do you get energy?**

   Do you prefer to focus on the external environment, the outer world, people, and activity? Or, do you prefer to focus on your own inner world of ideas and experiences? Do people energize you or do you get more energized with quiet time? Would you rather write or talk about your ideas? Do you prefer to learn by doing or by discussing or mental practice? Are you sociable or private?

2. **How do you take in information?**

   Are more of a detailed oriented person that focuses on what is actually happening, looking for practical realities? Or do you like to know the big picture and focus on relationships and connections, looking for patterns?

3. **How do you make decisions?**

   Do you prefer to focus on logical consequences of a choice or action, removing yourself from the situation and the people involved? Or do you prefer to consider what is important to you and the others involved in the decision?

4. **How do you deal with the outer world?**

   Do you prefer to live in a planned, orderly way seeking to regulate and manage your life? Or, do you prefer to live in a flexible, spontaneous way, seeking to experience and understand life rather than to control it? Is "sticking to a plan" important to you or would you rather stay open to new information and last-minute options?

There is no right or wrong with the answers to these questions. Each answer defines normal and valuable human behaviors. By answering questions like those above, using tools such as the Myers-Briggs Type Indicator, an individual and team can learn what personality type they have. Normally, people with similar personality types operate in a similar way, while others with different personality types operate differently. Again, when we are able to work as we prefer and enable others to work as they prefer, as a team we benefit from team members being at their best, feeling competent, natural, included, and energetic.

Flexibility to Get the Best of Everyone

If you're like me when I was an athlete, I really didn't like to stretch out. My flexibility wasn't great, so I basically hated to stretch, which then further hurt my flexibility. Not good. Anyway, in athletics, it is only helpful to be flexible and to maintain your flexibility physically. Likewise, if you are flexible in the positions you are able to play, you are more valuable to the team and give yourself a chance at more playing time. And, if you are flexible with the style of play by your coach and team, you are again more valuable to your team as they adjust to certain opponents and you are still able to perform as an individual.

Well, in the workplace, with much less concern for the physical flexibility (thank God), it's the same. Once you are self-aware of your personality, preferences, strengths, weaknesses, and so on, and once you are more aware of the same for your teammates and your team as a whole, one of the greatest skills and gifts you can give your team is the ability to flex your approach to best accommodate the team.

You may be somebody who prefers to push deadlines up until the last minute because that added pressure and resulting adrenaline brings out your best work. However, you may learn that most of your work team prefer to have the assignments complete a day ahead of the deadline. By sticking with your preferred approach, you will likely cause team dissension and stress and the issue will be about you and not the rest of the team. Being able to flex your preference in this case would not only help avoid added stress to your team, but would probably keep you from becoming a problem for the team.

Or, you may prefer to talk through problems and address them head on openly and directly until they are resolved. However, you know that the person with whom you are having problems is uncomfortable with face-to-face direct discussions about issues and prefers to write down thoughts and think privately before coming to a conclusion. In that case, it would be wise to find a happy medium approach that may be a mix of the two preferences to resolve the issues. On the other hand, if you know that another person has the same preferences as you, you can comfortably have the direct and open conversation without worrying about how the other person will take that approach.

Warning: With any tool, especially those that categorize people according to their characteristics, you must be careful not to assume that if a person is categorized as an X, then he or she will always do what X's do. Don't assume that all X's behave the same as all other X's all the time. Humans are humans and are unpredictable. And our best teammates are doing their best, as are we, to flex our preferences to be better teammates. Be careful not to limit people's greatness by the confines of any category or score that they've been assigned under any test.

Get to Know People to Get the Best of Everyone

As you can see, to get the best of everybody, one critical foundational element is simply to get to know as much as you can about each other. There are certainly limits when it comes to getting into personal lives in the workplace, but as it relates to the work that you do and the preferences of the team as to how that work can best be done, it is critical that you spend the time needed to understand how people think, how they manage conflict, how they handle change, how they prefer to get energy, make decisions, take in data and information, priorities on the job, and so on. From there, the best teams will work to create an environment that accommodates the preferences of those on the team so that they can bring their best to the team.

Value the Entire Team - A Christmas Story

Just after Thanksgiving in 2005, the Detroit Lions fired their head coach Steve Mariucci. It was more than unfortunate in many ways, but that is sometimes how it goes in professional sports. I've referenced Steve in a few places in this book as one of my role-models in my life, from my hometown, and this story illustrates one of the reasons why he has been a positive influence.

No matter where Steve worked during his coaching career, Northern Michigan University, Cal State Fullerton, Louisville, USC, Cal Berkeley, Green Bay Packers, San Francisco 49ers, or Detroit Lions, he made it a point to get to know as many of the organization as possible on a personal level. He would try to get to know the names of each member of the broader team, not only the players and coaches, but from the security guards, front office personnel, and administrative assistants, to the executives and the families of the owners. He would even buy each person working in the offices a Christmas gift during the Holiday Season.

So back to the Holiday Season of 2005, just after Thanksgiving. The General Manager was himself feeling intense pressure from Lions fans and the media to do something to account for another poor season, all suggesting that the GM may want to step down himself. So the GM decided to fire the head coach. Steve could have easily reacted negatively and selfishly, since he had only been given a couple seasons to turn the team around. He could have made negative statements to the media about the GM or the organization. Instead, he took the high road and continued to care about every other member of the organization. He recalls still having his building key even after being fired. So he continued his annual tradition and purchased his annual Christmas gift for every team member. And when the entire staff was attending their Holiday Party at another location, Steve entered the main office building and asked the security guard (who was his friend naturally) to help him get the gifts from his vehicle and pass them out to every desk in the building. Steve knew those people worked hard that year and he valued their contributions, despite the fact that they came up short on wins and losses and despite the fact that he was no longer the head coach of the team.

Tips to Get the Best of Everyone in the Workplace

To get the best of everybody in the workplace, consider the following:

- Respect everybody — all ages, genders, ethnicity, jobs, expertise, styles, preferences, etc.

- Know yourself — strengths, weaknesses, reputation, goals, motivation, triggers, etc.

- Be inclusive, get to know your workmates, and develop a sense of belonging for everyone

- Focus on what you and each workmate bring to the team vs. what you/they don't bring to the team

- Help build an environment where people can be at their best

Get the Best of Everyone in the Family

Families should be the place where getting the best of everyone is natural and easy. In theory, the family love should be able to look past the imperfections of each family member and each should love each other for who they are. Bringing out the best in each other should be a breeze. Right?

But doesn't it seem at times that the family is the most difficult place to bring out the best in everybody?

Did you ever notice that at times you treat your friends better than you treat your brother or sister? Did you ever find yourself treating your teachers, coaches, or boss better than you treat your parents? Did you ever catch yourself overlooking and not commenting on irritating behaviors from sports teammates and work colleagues, but not missing a heartbeat before laying into a brother, sister, child, or parent?

How can this be? We've just gone over the importance of sports teams and work teams getting to know each other and understanding each other's preferences, skills, abilities, and all of the other attributes that members of the team bring to the team. And then I spent time on the importance of being flexible to accommodate differences so that each team member can bring their best to the team.

Don't family members know each other better than anybody? Don't family members want what is best for the family naturally? Don't family members flex their own styles and preferences so that they can bring out the best in each family member?

I am clearly not a family therapist and will never claim to be, and I admit I don't have all the answers. But I want to be consistent with the format of this book within each lesson and I strongly believe that this topic is as important for families as it is for sports and the workplace. Wait, let me correct that. This topic is more important for families than it is for sports teams and the workplace. So as a family member since birth, a spouse for 30 years, a parent for 23+ years, and being a part of and working with teams for 40 years, I at least have an experienced opinion as to what might be happening with respect to this lesson in families.

Certainly, some families do in fact *Get the Best of Everybody* extremely well. A parent's unconditional love is real and there are millions of examples of self-sacrifice by family members who make better lives for others. I was blessed with a mother like that.

However, especially as we are growing up from a totally self-focused toddler, we can be extremely selfish and not even thinking about flexing our preferences and behaviors for other family members. We want and want and expect our parents, and even siblings, to give and give. As we mature to adolescence and then to young adulthood, we hopefully make that shift to focusing less on our own needs and more to the needs of the family.

In sports teams and especially in work teams, a big challenge is often that teammates don't know enough about each other. In families, perhaps we know each other too much. In sports and work teams, too often the success of the team doesn't matter to each individual as much as their own personal success. In families, especially for parents, the success (both perceived and real) may mean too much. In sports and work teams, relationships only go so far and are temporary; in families, relationships are as deep as they come and last forever. Families are a powder keg of emotion, which makes them both extra special and extra challenging.

Tips to Get the Best of Everyone in the Family

Again, I don't claim to have all the answers, especially when it comes to the complexities of families, but I do suggest applying some of the same principles that work in sports teams and in the workplace

To get the best of everybody in the family, consider the same, with minor tweaks:

- Respect everybody in the family

- Know yourself — strengths, weaknesses, reputation, goals, motivation, triggers, etc.

- Be inclusive and continually get to know your family as you grow together through time

- Focus on what you and each family member bring to the family vs. what you/they don't bring to the family. Pick your battles and focus on the greatness of your children, parents, and spouse. Bad hair will pass. Big mistakes will happen. Feelings will occasionally be hurt. Address the truly significant issues, but focus mostly on the good.

- Help build an environment where each family member can be at their best

Thought Leaders and Role Models for Getting the Best of Everyone

"An individual has not started living until he can rise above the narrow confines of his individualistic concerns to the broader concerns of all humanity."

— Martin Luther King, Jr.

"Sports are such a great teacher. I think of everything they've taught me: camaraderie, humility, how to resolve differences."

— Kobe Bryant

"Build for your team a feeling of oneness, of dependence on one another and of strength to be derived by unity."

— Vince Lombardi

"I can do things you cannot, you can do things I cannot; together we can do great things."

– St. Teresa of Calcutta

Your Choice: Will you strive to Get the Best of Everyone?

For What?

Before I go into Lesson #9, I first want to set the stage for why Lesson #9 is so important. A few years ago, I was at the height of my professional career, in my prime. My family was also doing well, healthy, succeeding in school, sports, and socially. Life was certainly good. For the most part, I was delivering on much of the 8 life lessons shared so far in this book.

But at the same time, I felt some emptiness in my heart. I couldn't exactly put a finger on why I wasn't fulfilled to the degree I wanted to be, and should have been. Something was missing and it had been missing for quite some time, perhaps most of my life. This is not a story of deep depression or hitting rock bottom before turning my life around. This is a more common and much less dramatic story of how "success" might not be what we think it is supposed to be.

During this period, I was sitting in the pews at my family church, and my pastor and friend, Fr. John Riccardo, an extremely gifted man of God who I've leaned on for help in this book and in my life, was speaking to our congregation at Our Lady of Good Counsel Parish in Plymouth, Michigan, a wealthy suburb outside of Detroit. He talked about how well-off our community was, noting the types of cars, restaurants, homes, clothes, hobbies, past-times, and beautiful churches. He talked also about the incredibly busy schedules that people had with careers, school activities, day care, sports, travel, and so on. He went on to acknowledge the stresses and hardships that challenge the lives of all of these "successful" people — at least successful in the eyes of the world.

Father John then shared how many people come to him every day with messed up lives, addiction, broken marriages, physical and mental illness exacerbated by stress, loneliness, despair, and even suicidal thoughts. He shared how he was trying to reconcile why, in such a beautiful community that seemed to have it all, that it would have so many underlying issues, and those issues seemed to be getting worse every year. Then Fr. John posed this powerful question to the entire congregation, in light of all the busy schedules, career pressures, social commitments, material possessions, and the pressures of the daily lives we have chosen. He simply said, "For what?" And he asked it again, "For what?" In that moment, I was generally happy with my life and could make the argument that I was quite "successful", so at first didn't even think the question was intended for me. Then it then struck me like being blindsided by a rushing defensive end that this question was being directed specifically to me.

Fr. John's question, "For what?" has led me to replacing the missing link in my life. His question resulted in several life decisions that my wife and I have made since that time that have brought us to the next stage of our lives and to another level of joy and fulfillment. I retired from my long career in the large corporate world, moved back near my small hometown near my parents and some of my closest childhood friends, began coaching high school football, and started writing this book. I thought God was leading my life before, but God has become THE guide in our lives and that has made the difference, replaced the missing link, and has brought more joy and peace to our lives. I still have my weak moments, moments of doubt, pride, and irritation with others, but that is rare these days as long as I focus on this important question, which I challenge you to always carry with you, "For What?", and always be comfortable with your answer.

The Parable of the Mexican Fisherman

To close out this section of the simple power of the "For What?" question, I share a wonderful little parable that I first heard when I lived in Mexico and which I've modified slightly to match my message in this important section of the book:

> An American investment banker was taking a much-needed vacation in a small coastal Mexican village when a small boat with just one fisherman docked. The boat had several large, fresh fish in it.
>
> The investment banker was impressed by the quality of the fish and asked the Mexican how long it took to catch them. The Mexican replied, "Only a little while."
>
> The banker then asked why he didn't stay out longer and catch more fish? The Mexican fisherman replied he had enough to support his family's immediate needs.
>
> The American then asked "But what do you do with the rest of your time?"

The Mexican fisherman replied, "I sleep late, fish a little, play with my children, take siesta with my wife, stroll into the village each evening where I sip wine and play guitar with my amigos: I am thankful to God for my full and busy life, señor."

The investment banker scoffed, "I am an Ivy League MBA, and I could help you. You could spend more time fishing and with the proceeds buy a bigger boat, and with the proceeds from the bigger boat you could buy several boats until eventually you would have a whole fleet of fishing boats. Instead of selling your catch to the middleman you could sell directly to the processor, eventually opening your own cannery. You could control the product, processing and distribution."

Then he added, "Of course, you would need to leave this small coastal fishing village and move to Mexico City where you would run your growing enterprise."

The Mexican fisherman asked, "But señor, how long will this all take?"

To which the American replied, "15-20 years."

"But what then? For what?" asked the Mexican.

The American laughed and said, "That's the best part. When the time is right you would announce an IPO and sell your company stock to the public and become very rich. You could make millions."

"Millions, señor? Then what? *For what?*"

To which the investment banker replied, "Then you would retire. You could move to a small coastal fishing village where you would sleep late, fish a little, play with your kids, take siesta with your wife, stroll to the village in the evenings where you could sip wine and play your guitar with your amigos."

With that in mind, let's go to the final lesson.

Lesson #9: God as Your Guide

To wrap up the 9 Lessons, in my experience and observation, all of what I just told you in every lesson thus far will certainly help you be a better athlete, more successful in your career, and be better with your family. However, without choosing God As Your Guide, I firmly believe that even those improvements will not be able to bring you the real success, fulfillment, and joy that you are in fact able to achieve by choosing God as Your Guide.

I know that this lesson may make some people feel uncomfortable, given the variety of belief systems out in the world. However, after decades of chasing success, with wide range of ups and downs, and now having abundant joy and peace in my life, please allow me to explain why I feel so strongly about this lesson being most important.

What Drives You?

To begin this lesson, ask yourself these questions:

Who or what is guiding my decisions on what is most important in my life, the master ruler of my life?

From where do I get my sense of wrong or right, good or bad, smart or foolish?

Who or what gives me clarity as to how I should act, what I should do, and who I should be in this world?

Those questions can be condensed to one: Who or what is my lord?

If you think deeply and honestly about this question, your answer may include one or more of the following forces:

- Popularity, notoriety, fame, headlines, social media followers
- Being different, image, me for me
- Boyfriend/girlfriend/spouse
- Political party or agenda
- Money, wealth, material possessions
- Career
- Partying, fun
- Sexuality
- Recognition, promotion, awards
- Sports, coaches
- Physical beauty

…and many other potential answers

If any of these forces, or several of them, are in fact your lord, driving your decisions and working as your master, then I am certain that you will not achieve the deep joy, satisfaction, and fulfillment in athletics, career, family, and life that you will experience with *God as Your Guide*.

I recall several periods throughout my life where my guide, my driver, and my motivation was not God, but instead was gaining notoriety, building a public image, making headlines, receiving awards, making more money, having more fun, and acquiring material possessions. And as I look back, those were most often the times when I was least fulfilled, least joyful, least fun to be around, and more confused as to what I wanted out of life.

Most of these forces are fleeting, coming and going quickly. Others are superficial, never fully attainable, and continually pressuring you to seek more and more, telling you that you are not enough, you haven't done enough, or you don't have enough. And most of these forces are based on fickle and wide ranging human opinions in one way or another, including your own opinions about yourself. People *will* let you down through these various forces that influence your decisions and actions; and you *will* even let yourself down at times in response to these forces.

Yet, regardless of our imperfections and mistakes, the perfect God will never let us down. He is a loving, forgiving, and fair God. He loves the imperfect you, loves those imperfect others, and expects us to love others as ourselves. To be more specific, in the person of Jesus Christ, God actually came from heaven, taught us how to live, and died for you and me so that we may be saved from death ourselves and instead have eternal life. *But to receive the gift of salvation and everlasting life, you must admit that you have made serious mistakes against God and others (that you are a sinner), you must recognize that Jesus Christ died and rose from the dead for you and your sins, and then you must deliberately choose God as Your Guide by accepting Jesus Christ as your Lord and do as He tells you - the master and ruler of your life forever.*

If you do this, you will have the joy of knowing the Lord God through His son Jesus Christ, with the power of the Holy Spirit — One God in three persons — and know His love in good times and in bad, in sickness and in health, until your human death when you more perfectly unite with Him in heaven. *You don't have to prove anything to God, just accept Him as your Lord, ask for His forgiveness for when you have let Him down, then choose to love and follow Him above all else in your heart and in every action.*

I commend all people who have achieved success in their sport, job, career, and family. However, this lesson is the missing link for many, the key to deep joy, fulfillment, satisfaction, and more happiness, as it was for me.

As St. John Paul II put it, *"What really matters in life is that we are loved by Christ and that we love Him in return. In comparison to the love of Jesus, everything else is secondary. And without the love of Jesus, everything else is useless."*

NFL Players With God as Their Guide

In a recent discussion with former NFL Head Coach for both the San Fransisco 49ers and Detroit Lions, Steve Mariucci, he told me how impressed he has been with a great number of NFL players with respect to their faith lives. Steve remembers back when he was a head coach and recalling the regimented weekly football season schedule which always had a prayer service with the team chaplain or a player, as well as a Catholic mass with a Catholic Priest, either on Saturday or Sunday depending on the game schedule. Bible study groups were common as well. He also had fond memories of when he was an assistant coach with the Green Bay Packers and recalls Hall of Fame defensive lineman and Christian pastor Reggie White leading a well-attended "players time" prayer service right in the locker room, even using shower space when needed. Steve told me that it was commonplace. The night before games and the day of games — before, during, and after the game. Players and coaches would pray in thanksgiving for their talents and opportunity to be a part of professional football, they would pray for safety during the on-field battle for their opponents, teammates, and themselves, and they would pray for the safety of all families and fans especially those who would travel to and from the games.

As an NFL Network analyst today, Steve continues to be impressed with many NFL players and coaches who have chosen God as Their Guide and are not ashamed to make that choice known to the public, whether it its simply to share their joy and/or to perhaps encourage others to do the same. These professional athletes have come to expect the prayer services, bible studies, and mass in their normal routine. For these gifted athletes, their faith is a critical element of their lives. They recognize that they have been blessed and are rightly glorifying God as their Lord and Savior in the midst of their highest level of success in their profession.

What About High School and College Student-Athletes?

Coach Mariucci and I also discussed our mutual concern that the younger athletes, and young people in general, especially in high school and college, don't seem to be making that same choice to the same degree. Yet, we recognize that is common as well. That is an age for many to be searching for who they really are and are still maturing, not always making the best life choices. It happened to me as well at that age, and became one of the few periods of regret in my life from a spiritual development perspective. I enjoyed the freedom to do what I wanted for the most part, with the focus on having fun, partying, drinking, and staying shallow with relationships, especially with the girls I would date. Instead of growing in my faith and relationship with God, I sort of ignored it and Him, because to avoid facing God wouldn't remind me of the poor choices I was making during that time. And when I would go to church to attend mass, I knew I was being hypocritical in how I was living when compared with what I espoused as my beliefs. I recall Tony Dungy, the legendary former NFL football player and coach of the Indianapolis Colts, say that his only regret was that he didn't grow spiritually until after college; he viewed his time up until then as wasted time relative to the Lord.[26] I feel the same. Fortunately, we have a forgiving God and it is never too late to turn one's life around and regain at least some of that lost time.

Wildcats and Tigers — Real Winning

But I don't want to suggest you can't find those in collegiate athletics who have chosen God as their guide. Many have in fact done so. I was blessed to have such a coach in my college days, Coach Herb Grenke of the Northern Michigan

---

[26] Arise With The Guys 2020 annual conference (video broadcast)

University Football Wildcats of the 1980s, who led our weekly optional prayer service in a public university. And even though I was being shallow and lazy with my spiritual development at that time in my young life, Coach made it clear that this was a priority for him and he encouraged all of us to do the same, regardless of wins and losses.

Today, I can't help but get pumped up when I think about one collegiate football coach in particular who chose God as his guide as a young athlete and has carried that choice through to being one of the most successful college football coaches in history. In a recent podcast called, "Huddle Up! Coaches Edition,"[27] newly retired NFL football star and man of true character and strong faith, Ben Watson, along his wife Kirsten, interviewed Tony Dungy (who I've leaned on a few times already in this book as a role-model) and Dabo Swinney, head coach of the Clemson Tigers, along with his wife Kathleen. In the interview, Coach Swinney talked about the impact he has been able to have on young people by allowing God work through him as he coaches football, allowing God to be his guide in his career, in the way he recruits, the way he coaches, and who he is. With God as his guide, he shared that God also challenges him to be bold and to stay focused on what is most important at all times. He explained that no matter how much he loves his job and wants to win football games (and he certainly does both of those), he places faith and family above football and encourages his staff, players, and anybody who listens to his messages to do the same. And as a powerful capper to his messages in the interview that day,

---

[27] https://www.youtube.com/watch?v=io2mXye6Fbs

he said something that felt especially pertinent to what I've shared in this book, and completely aligned with my lifetime of experiences and observations. Coach Dabo said:

> *"So many people today are afraid of criticism, afraid of not being politically correct or whatever it may be. There's a lot of hostility toward Christianity today. But I always tell people that the hope of the world — it's not in politics, it's not in a new president, it's not in a stimulus package, it's not in anything — the hope of the world is Jesus. It always has been, always will be. It's not Nike, not Instagram,…not our bank accounts, not our college teams. The hope of the world comes from a relationship with Jesus. And that's what I know, and I've known that for a long time. I've just tried to live my life in a way that hopefully can glorify Him, but more importantly can be a light to others who are in the darkness."*

Whether the Clemson Tigers have won the national championship or lost the national championship, it's no surprise to me that their coach and several key players first glorify God as their guide when interviewed by reporters following the game - win or lose.

I encourage you to pick role models that have made the choice to have God as Their Guide and deeply consider doing the same thing yourself if you have not already done so. The people I just mentioned and others who I've referenced throughout this book are some to keep an eye on. But you find the ones that fit your style, who may fire you up and show you ways to be the best version of yourself.

Lesson #9 Enables Every Other Lesson

To further explain why Lesson #9: God as Your Guide is the most important of these nine lessons, I'm going to show how choosing "God as Your Guide" enables every other lesson covered in this book.

In each lesson of this book so far, I've used quotes from famous thought leaders and role models, some of history's most recognized athletes, scientists, philosophers, political leaders, and others who are viewed as successful in their respective areas of expertise and for their notoriety. In this section, I'll quote from sacred scripture and from a few prominent people who have in fact chosen God as their guide and, as a result, found deep fulfillment and joy in their lives. The guidance given to us from the Holy Bible is inspired by God and has been shared through others for thousands of years, giving us clear direction from our Lord and from those He chose to use as instruments of his peace and joy.

The advice from the world's most successful people are certainly helpful. However, I encourage you to pay even closer attention to the words and advice from the Creator of the Universe and those who have chosen Him to be the driving force in their lives. I'll only share a splinter of what is contained in sacred scripture, but I am confident that it will be powerful and am hopeful that this can spark a deeper interest in you to read sacred scripture as a habit and use it as a guide for your life.

For starters, Jesus himself, in the Gospel of Matthew (6:33), when he was counseling people not to worry so much about what they were going to eat or drink, or what clothes they were going to wear, said, *"But seek first His kingdom and His righteousness, and all these things will be given to you as well."*

So how does God as Your Guide enable all other lessons? Let's take a quick look, lesson by lesson.

Lesson #9 Enables Lesson #1: Be Coachable

Humility is at the core of being coachable. Without the humility to be able to see your own faults, to be open to the observations of another, to be willing to change your ways, you simply will not be coachable. As Jesus Christ and others who have chosen God as their guide have put it:

In the gospel of Luke (18:14), Jesus tells us, *"For everyone who exalts himself will be humbled, but the one who humbles himself will be exalted."*

In the gospel of Matthew (18:4) Jesus encourages us to be humble like children, *"Whoever humbles himself like this child is the greatest in the kingdom of heaven."*

St. Peter gives similar advice with, *"In the same way, you who are younger, submit yourselves to your elders. All of you, clothe yourselves with humility toward one another, because, 'God opposes the proud but shows favor to the humble.'" (1 Peter 5:5)*

And in the Book of Proverbs, humility for the purpose of learning is addressed several times, including:

"When pride comes, then comes disgrace, but with humility comes wisdom." (Proverbs 11:2)

"The way of fools seems right to them, but the wise listen to advice." (Proverbs 12:15)

"Let someone else praise you, and not your own mouth; an outsider, and not your own lips." (Proverbs 27:2)

John the Baptist was one of the most popular preachers in the first century. He had crowds of people following him, considering him among the greatest of prophets, and his rockstar popularity was growing by the day. But as soon as Jesus came onto the scene to begin His ministry, John the Baptist immediately humbled himself, saying, *"He must increase, I must decrease." (John 3:30)*

So with a humble spirit, one can be authentically coachable. When you are humble, you can then be docile — which is a state of mind ready to learn. When you are humble and docile, you will be coachable. When coachable, it is never too late to turn things around and you are able to grow continually. Most importantly, you will be able to enjoy life everlasting.

Choose God as Your Guide and you will Be Coachable.

Lesson #9 Enables Lesson #2: Be a Great Teammate

At the heart of being a great teammate is being unselfish, being able to shift your focus away from yourself and toward your teammates. As a great teammate, you will be there for your teammates when they fall off the path, keeping them out of trouble, picking them up when they fall. The more you can do this, the better teammate you will become.

Jesus taught us to be the ultimate teammates by imploring us, as he said in the gospel of Mark (12:31), to *"Love your neighbor as yourself."*

In St. Paul's letter to the Philippians (2:3), St. Paul reinforces Jesus' message, *"Do nothing from selfishness or empty conceit, but with humility of mind regard one another as more important than yourselves."*

And further explains in his first letter to the Corinthians, *"Love is patient, love is kind. Love does not envy, love does not boast, it is not proud. It does not dishonor others, it is not self-seeking, it is not easily angered, it keeps no record of wrongs." (1 Corinthians 13:4-5)*

God assures us of the benefits of being a great teammate in Proverbs 11:25, *"A generous person will prosper; whoever refreshes others will be refreshed."*

But on the other hand, we are warned in James 3:16, *"For where you have envy and selfish ambition, there you find disorder and every evil practice."*

Jesus taught us the sign of the ultimate teammate in the Gospel of John 15:13, *"Greater love has no one than this, that one lay down his life for his friends."*

When you think about the **greatest teammate of all times**, the one who literally gave up his life for 'the team' — the team of all of humanity — and did so under the most brutal circumstances, you have the perfect role model, Jesus Christ. He is the ultimate teammate who gave His everything for each one of us. He is always there for us through the wins, losses, easy days, and tough days. He will never let us down if we simply allow Him to be our teammate and we to be his teammate. And although you'll never achieve that level of perfection, you can at least give every effort to be as close as possible to being a teammate like Christ, to endure pain & suffering, to love even when not loved yourself, to rise above the desire to give up, all for the success and honor of your team — your teammates, and your ultimate Coach (God the Father).

Choose God as Your Guide to Be a Great Teammate.

Lesson #9 Enables Lesson #3: Play Your Position Well

Playing Your Position Well requires being fully aware of your strengths and weaknesses so you can focus on **what you can control** — which is **your effort and your attitude.** Your focus can't be on your coach, your teammates, your siblings, your teachers, your boss, or your parents.

Jesus challenged us in the Gospel of Matthew (7:3-5) to look first at ourselves rather than worrying about others' faults when he asked:

> *"Why do you see the speck that is in your brother's eye, but do not notice the log that is in your own eye? Or how can you say to your brother, 'Let me take the speck out of your eye,' when there is the log in your own eye? You hypocrite, first take the log out of your own eye, and then you will see clearly to take the spec out of your brother's eye."*

Through St. Paul, who chose God as His Guide over 2,000 years ago, we have inspired direction from God on attitude and effort, including in his letters below:

> *"Do all things without grumbling or questioning, that you may be blameless and innocent, children of God without blemish in the midst of a crooked and twisted generation, among whom you shine as lights in the world." (Philippians 2:14-15)*

> *"And let us not grow weary of doing good, for in due season we will reap, if we do not give up." (Galatians 6:9)*

Giving Your Talents Back to God Joyfully

In order to be able to focus on what you can control (again, effort and attitude), I encourage you to first recognize the gifts you have been given in your life and then give those gifts back to God in how you use them. You've been blessed with the ability to play sports, to go to school, to have friends, to learn, to work, to have fun, to be part of a family. These are gifts from God. When you approach anything that you do with the mindset of giving back to God what he gave you in the form of opportunity, skills, people in your life, nature, and even challenges — everything — then you will be able to approach every day at practice, work, or in your family (good and bad days) with the joy of knowing you are giving back and serving God by serving others.

In his letter to the Colossians (3:23-24), St. Paul frames any job as one that is serving God, *"Whatever you do, work heartily, as for the Lord and not for men, knowing that from the Lord you will receive the inheritance as your reward. You are serving the Lord Christ."*

And in his letter to the Corinthians (1 Corinthians 10:31), St. Paul says, *"So, whether you eat or drink, or whatever you do, do all to the glory of God."*

Choose God as Your Guide to Play Your Positions Well.

Lesson #9 Enables Lesson #4: Master Adversity

For no other lesson does *God as Your Guide* enable more than *Lesson #4: Master Adversity*. So I'll take extra care to lay out why this is so.

Suffering is Part of Life

The first enabler to mastering adversity is to **recognize that suffering is a part of life and that God has given you all that you need** to get through anything that comes your way. God allows pain and suffering. He doesn't create pain and suffering, but allows it in order to enable those with faith in

Him even deeper appreciation for the good in the world, the good that often comes as a result of tragedy and failure.

When the apostles of Jesus found themselves terrified in the middle of a torrential storm while at sea, they screamed out to Jesus and begged for help. They started to doubt whether Jesus cared about them. So Jesus calmly quieted the storm and replied, *"Why are you so afraid? Do you still have no faith?"* *(Mark 4:40).* These questions, the calming power of Jesus, and faith in Him, are the bedrock of Mastering Adversity.

St. Paul confidently expresses his source of strength and ability to master adversity in his letter to the Philippians (4:13), *"I can do all things through Him who strengthens me."*

The angel Gabriel assured Mary, the Blessed Mother of Jesus, that she can rest assured and be confident in dealing with all challenges, *"For nothing will be impossible for God." Luke (1:37).*

Forgiveness

The second enabler to mastering adversity to be able to overcome any obstacle in our lives is the gift from our Lord God called *forgiveness.* This is especially powerful when we are the one that has messed up personally, when we have blown it with our actions or our inaction, when we have let the team down by being selfish, for wanting more for ourselves than for the team, for our own glory and recognition, or through our own laziness at the expense of the team. We may have spread rumors about a teammate or created unhealthy cliques among the team, playing favorites on or off the field of play or in the workplace, or not doing our own job well due to lack of preparation or lack of effort, or even worse cheating. And as a result, we hurt the team, our family, and ourself. We are human; that happens.

But, with the gift of forgiveness, no matter how bad our actions or inaction have been, no matter the consequences, we can start fresh. If we admit our mistakes and ask for forgiveness from our Lord, and then do our best to reconcile with those we've hurt, we will be forgiven. And as a team or family, if one of your teammates or family members has hurt the team or family and asks for forgiveness, you must forgive, as our God forgives you. We truly can start fresh in the eyes of God. We may not forget what we did wrong, which is ok, but with the power of knowing we are in fact forgiven, we can in fact master adversity.

Jesus himself instructed us, *"If your brother or sister sins against you, rebuke them; and if they repent, forgive them. Even if they sin against you seven times in a day and seven times come back to you saying 'I repent,' you must forgive them." (Luke 17:3-4)*

And several passages in sacred scripture give us clarity about forgiveness and how it can enable us to master adversity, including:

> *"Repent, then, and turn to God, so that your sins may be wiped out, that times of refreshing may come from the Lord." (Acts 3:19)*

> *"And when you stand praying, if you hold anything against anyone, forgive them, so that your Father in heaven may forgive you your sins." (Mark 11:25)*

> *"Get rid of all bitterness, rage and anger, brawling and slander, along with every form of malice. Be kind and compassionate to one*

another, forgiving each other, just as in Christ God forgave you." (Ephesians 4:31-32)

Faith

A third enabler to mastering adversity, and the most powerful, is faith, faith in knowing God, knowing that He is the one in control, and trusting Him to help get you through any adversity in your life. And with this faith, you shall not be afraid.

My friend and a spiritual mentor, Fr. John Riccardo, former pastor at Our Lady of Good Counsel parish in Plymouth, Michigan, and now the Executive Director of *Acts XXIX*, a non-profit organization that strengthens churches throughout the country, shared with me what he referred to as the best visual image for faith he had ever heard. He told me this way:

"Faith is to lean so far over on God that if He wasn't there you'd fall down."

He went on to explain:

Faith is relational. In other words, faith is about trust, not about some kind of mere intellectual assent. This is a familiar concept for athletes and professionals to understand due to the people in their lives on whom trust is placed. Whether it's with a strength and conditioning coach, a golf coach, a football coach, Usain Bolt's coach (the example used in Lesson #1: Be Coachable), a financial planner, or an executive coach, athletes and professionals REGULARLY entrust themselves to others so as to become great. They do this with people who have demonstrated (at least in theory) that they are worthy of trust. No one (!) is worthy of our trust like Jesus is, for He has proven it by laying down his life..."

And just as Jesus asked his own closest friends in the middle of a violent storm, He asks us, in the middle of our own terrible and not-so-terrible storms, *"Why are you so afraid? Have you still no faith?" (Mark 4:40)*

God as Your Guide Through A Pandemic

Thinking more about the coronavirus with regard to mastering adversity. Having 'God as Your Guide' throughout the coronavirus experience enabled many faithful to not only cope with this time of fear, suffering, and death, but to rise above the fear to help their neighbors, to sacrifice self-interests, to accept and work through financial burdens, and to share the Good News of Jesus Christ, by kind words, encouragement, appropriate humor, and through selfless deeds.

And as I watched the pandemic worsen and the world's reactions to it, I prayed, observed people, and experienced my own feelings of surprise, concern, fear, anger, and at the same time gratefulness for being safe and healthy during difficult times. I couldn't help but wonder that although God doesn't want pain and suffering, He allowed the coronavirus pandemic to occur during a time when the U.S. was at one of its most divided in history, when other countries were pitted against each other for economic, social, military, or political reasons, at a time when the political environment had people hating certain politicians and any of their followers, a time when media exacerbated the differences, disagreements, and negativity among people instead of driving unity and common good, when social media has replaced relatively respectful intelligent debate with "take the gloves off" immature and often vulgar virtual fighting.

As Pope Francis said in his sermon to an empty St. Peter's Square, in Rome Italy, in the midst of the coronavirus pandemic on March 27, 2020:

> *"The storm exposes our vulnerability and uncovers those false and superfluous certainties around which we have constructed our daily schedules, our projects, our habits and priorities. It shows us how we have allowed to become dull and feeble the very things that nourish, sustain and strengthen our lives and our communities. The tempest lays bare all our prepackaged ideas and forgetfulness of what nourishes our people's souls; all those attempts that anesthetize us with ways of thinking and acting that supposedly save us, but instead prove incapable of putting us in touch with our roots and keeping alive the memory of those who have gone before us. We deprive ourselves of the antibodies we need to confront adversity....."*

> *"...In the face of so much suffering, where the authentic development of our peoples is assessed, we experience the priestly prayer of Jesus: "That they may all be one" (Jn 17:21). How many people every day are exercising patience and offering hope, taking care to sow not panic but a shared responsibility. How many fathers, mothers, grandparents and teachers are showing our children, in small everyday gestures, how to face up to and navigate a crisis by adjusting their routines, lifting their gaze and fostering prayer. How many are praying, offering and interceding for the good of all. Prayer and quiet service: these are our victorious weapons."*[28]

---

[28]https://aleteia.org/2020/03/27/full-text-from-pope-francis-homily-for-the-special-urbi-et-orbi-blessing/

As horrible as the virus and its impact has been for many people and families, it was encouraging to see many in the world come together in prayer, empathy, and in a coordinated manner to take the actions necessary to stop this invisible enemy and to help their neighbors. Heroic individuals, organizations, private companies, and certain civic leaders emerged through the darkness of fear and hate as beacons of light, as selfless warriors for what is good in the world. Families spent quality time together, home schooling, hiking, reading, writing, and praying. Churches and churchgoers were forced to reimagine ways to continue sharing the Good News and continuing sacred traditions. I would never wish tragedy upon anybody, but in the face of human tragedy, if we can keep our eyes fixed on our Lord Jesus Christ, we will not grow weary, we will not lose heart, and we not only survive in the flesh, but we will thrive spiritually. Joy in the face of adversity is ours to have.

St. Teresa of Calcutta left us with a thought that might feel closer to us in light of the pandemic, *"You will never truly realize God is all you need until He becomes all you have."* [29]

The old priest and scribe in Old Testament, Ezra, thousands of years ago, said to his fellow citizens who were fearful of their challenging times and had been regretting not choosing God as Their Guide, *"And do not be grieved, for the joy of the Lord is your strength."* (Nehemiah 8:10).

The prophet Isaiah was inspired by the Holy Spirit to put God's word's this way, *"For I am the Lord, your God, who grasp your right hand; It is I who say to you, Do not fear, I will help you."* (Isaiah 41:13)

---

[29] https://everydaypower.com/quotes-by-mother-teresa/

And finally, perhaps most clearly, when faced with a pending certain torturous death, Jesus said to his closest friends, and in doing so also says to us:

> *"Peace I leave with you; my peace I give you. Not as the world gives do I give to you. Let not your hearts be troubled, neither let them be afraid." (John 14:27)*

> *"I have told you this so that you might have peace in me. In the world you will have trouble, but take courage, I have conquered the world." (John 16:33)*

Build Your House on The Rock

To master adversity, Jesus has given us a clear image in the gospel of Matthew 7:24-27, when he said:

> *"Everyone then who hears these words of mine and does them will be like a wise man who built his house on the rock. And the rain fell, and the floods came, and the winds blew and beat on that house, but it did not fall, because it had been founded on the rock. And everyone who hears these words of mine and does not do them will be like a foolish man who build his house on the sand. And the rain fell, and the floods came, and the winds blew and beat against that house, and it fell, and great was the fall of it."*

The storms will come. Build your house on a rock before they hit. For if you wait for the storm to begin building on the rock, your house will fall.

God as Your Guide in the Face of Adversity

Demario Davis is an All-Pro NFL veteran linebacker and spoke recently at the "Arise with the Guys" conference that I watched online during the COVID-19 stay-at-home orders. Demario explained,

> "...*during adverse times, what you stand on and your foundation becomes most important. When the virus became a pandemic... something that was touching our entire world and was unprecedented, it sent me right back to praying with God and spending time with my Word. And the more and more I looked at it, the more encouraged I got because a crisis is nothing new to God. This isn't something that is unique to Him. He's been a part of every crisis that has ever touched, what people thought was a crisis, that has ever touched the earth, He has been a part of it. He's not surprised by it. And the confident word that I got, that I've been standing on is, one, he encouraged me to stop looking at the world and focus my attention on Him. It also taught me to seek Him for the answers that I'm looking for and so I go to His word to seek His advice as to what to do during these times, and then to just stand on His promises. And one of His great promises is Romans 8:28, 'all things work together for good, for those who are called according to his purpose.' So though this looks like a very dire situation, we know that it is going to work together for good, that He is ultimately going to get the most glory for it. And that's what it's about. That is the story of this Bible that everything works for His glory. I don't know how He is going to get glory from this, but I know that He is going to get glory from it and that's the promise that I'm standing on. And that gives me hope. That gives my family hope. And so, though this situation could be very stressful, His word gives me a deep peace that I can have for myself, for my wife and my children, and for other people we influence."*

Demario went on to give valuable advice to young people with,

> *"What's given me confidence and peace is my relationship with God, which I developed in 2008….Focus on your relationship with God. …When you're built on a steady foundation, no matter what comes you won't be swayed…I encourage everybody to have that [relationship with God]. Find that."*

Two-time All-Pro NFL quarterback **Kirk Cousins**, who also spoke at the 2020 "Arise with the Guys" conference encouraged especially young people during any tough time, including the COVID-19 pandemic, to read Proverbs 3:5-6, which says:

> *"Trust in the Lord with all your heart, and do not lean on your own understanding. In all your ways acknowledge him, and he will make straight your paths."*

Kirk encouraged young people to:

> *"…claim that verse, memorize it, pray that verse, and watch God show up time and again in your life. And I think you'll be able to look back a few years from now and see how God used this time to bring you exactly to where he wanted you. God is not surprised by this virus and he has a plan for your life and He's going to accomplish those plans. Our job is to trust and obey Him and let Him handle the rest."*

Choose God as Your Guide and you will be able to Master Adversity.

Lesson #9 Enables Lesson #5: Peak Performance State

With God as Your Guide, you will enhance your approach to getting into and maintaining your Peak Performance State.

The Ultimate Role Model

In Lesson #5, I encouraged you to pick role models in athletics, your profession, and even to look around for role model families in order to learn and to be inspired. Now I turn to the ultimate example of preparation, our Lord Jesus Christ. Jesus came to this earth with one mission — a very difficult mission. He prepared mentally, physically, and emotionally to complete his mission. He studied, observed people and situations, fasted for 40 days at one time, prayed intensely, built relationships with his team, everything He did was in preparation to suffer a most horrible death and to rise again so that we may have eternal life.

So as you consider role models for working through the pain and challenge of preparation for your mission on earth, think about how St. Paul put it in his letter to the Hebrews:

> *"Therefore, since we are surrounded by such a great cloud of witnesses, let us throw off everything that hinders and the sin that so easily entangles. And let us run with perseverance the race marked out for us, fixing our eyes on Jesus, the pioneer and perfecter of faith. For the joy set before him he endured the cross, scorning its shame, and sat down at the right hand of the throne of God. Consider him who endured such opposition from sinners, so that you will not grow weary and lose heart." (Hebrews 12:1-3)*

Physical

"Do you not know that your bodies are temples of the Holy Spirit, who is in you, whom you have received from God? You are not your own; you were bought at a price. Therefore honor God with your bodies." (1 Corinthians 6:19-20)

Mental

"The fear of the Lord is the beginning of wisdom; and the knowledge of the Holy One is Insight." (Proverbs 9:10)

Emotional

"A cheerful heart is good medicine, but a crushed spirit dries up the bones." (Proverbs 17:22)

"Do not be anxious about anything, but in everything by prayer and supplication with thanksgiving let your requests be made known to God. And the peace of God, which surpasses all understanding, will guard your hearts and your minds in Christ Jesus." (Philippians 4:6-7)

Choose God as Your Guide and you will be able to achieve and maintain Peak Performance State.

Lesson #9 Enables Lesson #6: Bias for Action

Choosing God as Your Guide will help you break through many of the obstacles that prevent progress and inspire you to get the right things done.

Talk is Cheap

Sacred scripture provides direction for taking action, not simply talking or listening. To touch on only a few, look in the book of James 1:22, where it is written, *"But be doers of the Word, and not hearers only, deceiving yourselves."* And again in the first letter of John, *"Little children, let us not love in word or talk but in deed and in truth." (1 John 3:18)* And then again in Proverbs 14:23, *"In all toil there is profit, but mere talk tends only to poverty."*

Fear

At the base of indecision often lies fear, fear of being wrong, fear of being criticized, fear of a damaged reputation, fear of losing, or other fear. When our faith is weak, we are easily frightened.

But, if you are able to accept God as Your Guide, Psalm 27:1 would be your rallying cry and your mindset, *"The Lord is my light and my salvation; whom shall I fear? The Lord is the stronghold of my life; of whom shall I be afraid?"*

Or in Deuteronomy 31:8, *"He will never leave you nor forsake you. Do not be afraid; do not be discouraged."*

At Least Ask

And still further, Jesus himself encourages us to act by simply asking for what we want in the gospel of Luke (11:9-10), *"And I tell you, ask, and it will be given to you; seek, and you will find; knock, and it will be opened to you. For everyone who asks receives, and the one who seeks finds, and to the one who knocks it will be opened."*

Choose God as Your Guide and you will develop a Bias for Action.

Lesson #9 Enables Lesson #7: Discipline as a Habit

At the heart of *Discipline As a Habit* is knowing your **top priority** before deciding what is most important to do and when that should be done. You have so many competing priorities and we all can easily get overwhelmed with too much to do in any one day or at any one time. You want to have good friends, get good grades, make money, be successful in your athletics, have fun, have followers on social media, be charitable, learn a musical instrument, on and on. The list can be endless.

But if you one you recognize and decide that your top priority is loving God above all else, having God as your Guide, you can more easily whittle down your list of actions to a more manageable level. Yes, you can still try to jam more in than you should, but God doesn't want you to do more. He wants you to do what is right and spend time with Him. Further, as explained in sacred scripture in multiple places, God gives you all the strength, knowledge, and clarity you need to form discipline as a habit in your life. If you are ever in doubt as to knowing what you should do and when you should do it, take it to God in prayer. Make Him a priority in your schedule. Take the time to learn what I'm touching on in this Lesson #9: God as Your Guide, by reading the Bible and other spiritual teachings.

Once you have your priorities straight, then you are able to focus on **what** you know you should do, **when** you should do it, whether you **like it or not**. This still won't be easy at times, but again, God gives us the advice and insights through sacred scripture that enables us to develop Discipline as a Habit.

Philippians 4:13: "I can do all things through him who strengthens me."

Hebrews 12:11: "For the moment all discipline seems painful rather than pleasant, but later it yields the peaceful fruit of righteousness to those who have been trained by it.'

Proverbs 13:4: "The soul of the sluggard craves and gets nothing, while the soul of the diligent is richly supplied."

2 Chronicles 15:7: But you, take courage! Do not let your hands be weak, for your work shall be rewarded."

Chose God as Your Guide to develop Discipline as a Habit.

Lesson #9 Enables Lesson #8: Best of Everyone

To be able to get the best of everyone, you must first develop the ability to *appreciate everyone, to even go as far as to love everyone.* This doesn't mean you have to love everything about everyone, but unless you develop the ability to love others, despite your & their differences, you will be held back from getting the best from everyone.

At a young age, I was taught by my dad, affectionately known as **Sugar Popp** that *nobody is better than you, but you're no better than anybody else.* It was some of the best advice I had ever received, given its simplicity and clarity of how I compared with every other person in the universe — from the most talented and famous to the least talented and unknown. On one hand, it is motivational advice, giving me the confidence to compete in sports, finding a job, dealing with high-ranking members of society, and in any situation where I need to compete or otherwise deal with potentially intimidating people in this super-talented world. On the other hand, this advice is humbling for the times I even start to think that I'm better than anybody based on my own flawed human assessment of "better" when it comes to people. I encourage you, based on the guidance above, to always hold those two thoughts together, at the same time, and with equal weight, in order to help you first love God, the One who loves you as much as anybody in the world, to also love yourself (but not too much), and allow that, in turn, to enable you to love others as yourself and as God loves you.

Let us again look at what sacred scripture has to say, this time about getting the best of everyone.

In the gospel of Mark (12:31), Jesus gives us the most simple but fundamental command, *"You shall love your neighbor as yourself."*

> In the Letter of St. Paul to the Philippians 2:3-4, St. Paul advises, *"Do nothing out of selfish ambition or vain conceit. Rather, in humility value others above yourselves, not looking to your own interests but each of you to the interests of the others."*

> In St. Pauls First Letter to the Corinthians (12:20-27), he says, *"As it is, there are many parts, but one body. The eye cannot say to the hand, 'don't need you!' And the head cannot say to the feet, 'I don't need you!' On the contrary, those parts of the body that seem to be weaker are indispensable, and the parts that we*

think are less honorable we treat with special honor. And the parts that are unpresentable are treated with special modesty, while our presentable parts need no special treatment. But God has put the body together, giving greater honor to the parts that lacked it, so that there should be no division in the body, but that its parts should have equal concern for each other. If one part suffers, every part suffers with it; if one part is honored, every part rejoices with it. Now you are the body of Christ, and each one of you is a part of it."

St. Teresa of Calcutta puts it beautifully, *"You can love all men perfectly if you love the one God in them all."*

And regarding the concept of "belonging" which I referenced in Lesson #8 as important to getting the best of everyone, the following should give us peace of mind that we "belong" at all times and in all situations in the right place, regardless of the difficulties of life:

"But you belong to God, my dear children. You have already won a victory over those people, because the Spirit who lives in you is greater than the spirit who lives in the world." (1 John 4:4)

"See how much the Father has loved us! His love is so great that we are called God's children—and so, in fact, we are. This is why the world does not know us: it has not known God." — (1 John 3:1)

Choose God as Your Guide and you can Get the Best of Everyone including <u>Yourself</u>!

Lesson #9 Summary

This was a longer section of the book, so let me summarize the main points of Lesson #9: God as Your Guide and how it enables every other lesson.

■ Ask yourself what drives your biggest decisions in life, **"Who or what is my lord?"** Choosing God as your Lord is the only lasting reliable choice.

■ Stop trying to satisfy people and their fickle definition of "success." You don't have to prove anything to God, just love Him as He loves you.

■ Many successful people, including professional athletes and successful business people have chosen God as Their Guide. Keep an eye on the right role models in your life.

■ Choosing God as your guide enables every other lesson in this book. If it were easy to live these lessons, everybody would be expert in every one of them. **You can't do it all alone, so follow His guidance, ask for and use His help for each lesson.**

Lesson 1: Humility is at the core of *Being Coachable*

Lesson 2: Loving your neighbor as yourself is the key to *Be a Great Teammate*

Lesson 3: Recognizing the gifts that God has given you and that you serve and glorify God in your work is the sure way to *Play Your Position(s) Well*

Lesson 4: To *Master Adversity:*

- Recognize that suffering is a part of life and that God has given you all that you need to get through anything that comes your way

- Learn to forgive and be forgiven, this is a beautiful gift from God

- Build your house on a rock *before* the winds blow to withstand any storm

- Above all, have Faith in knowing and trusting God

Lesson 5: To achieve *Peak Performance State:*

- See Jesus as the ultimate role model of preparation for a mission

- Treat your body as a temple of the Holy Spirit

- Build both knowledge of and a healthy fear of the Lord

- Be anxious about nothing through the peace of knowing God

Lesson 6: To build a *Bias for Action:*

- At least ask our Lord for what you seek

- Avoid simply talking or only listening, do the right things now

- Be not afraid

Lesson 7: To develop *Discipline As a Habit:*

- Prayerfully establish your true top priorities in life

- Recognize that God is with you and strengthens you as you do what is right

- Find motivation in the promise of everlasting reward

Lesson 8: To *Get the Best of Everyone:*

- Love your neighbor as yourself, recognizing that we are all part of one body

- See God in each person and see the best in each of His creations

- Remember that nobody is better than you and you're no better than anybody else

- Love God first, love others as God loves you, and love yourself

Choose God as Your Guide and allow Him to help you truly Be Successful.

"Success" vs. Success

I started off this book with a little background on my athletic career, professional experience, and family, sharing what can be considered success — undefeated seasons, post-season awards and recognition, Sports Hall of Fame, promotions, lofty titles, highly paid, retiring at a relatively young age, and so on. In addition, I have known, played sports with, worked with, and have observed and researched many "successful" people over my lifetime who have achieved way more than I have, some who have become world-class professional athletes, super-wealthy business people, famous actors, civic leaders, media personalities, distinguished doctors, prominent lawyers, noted scientists, and so on. Several of them are mentioned and quoted throughout this book. They are all to be commended for their accomplishments and we can learn a tremendous amount from their words and actions.

However, as I look around, I also see many so-called "successful" people in the world who are empty, unhappy, or have something missing in their lives that is keeping them from being fulfilled and experiencing deep joy. Throughout history and in the news on just about a daily basis, we see examples of the all-too-common heart-wrenching stories of the seemingly successful person whose life is a mess. Despite the appearance of having it all and being "successful," we instead see broken families, fits of anger, hostility, dissension, envy, rivalries, drug addictions and even suicide. These aren't

226

the fruits of success. The stories we see less often, but also tragic are those who are doing *fine*, but have that missing link in their lives that prevents them from deep joy and fulfillment — which was my experience. These too are sad stories because quite often the feeling of *fine* isn't enough of a push or motivation to take action to change anything and therefore prevents the achievement of deeper fulfillment and profound joy in life.

Regardless of whether one's story is that of a deeply troubling tragedy or one less tragic but more typical, I have found that **"Success" is the biggest opponent of Success.** "Success" with quotation marks is that which is defined in the eyes of the world vs. **real success** which brings the deeper fulfillment and joy, that which lies deep inside our souls waiting to be tapped, regardless of trophies, awards, and honors. **That is the greatest competition of human existence today — "Success" vs. Success, the game of life and the Game of a Lifetime.**

I challenge you to think deeply and perhaps differently about success. **Real success goes beyond what I described at the beginning of this book.** Real success is not defined as the number of games you win, the accomplishments you achieve, the awards you may or may not receive, the career you choose, the money you make, the house you live in, the car you drive, fame, or the recognition you receive from other people. Often, these achievements are impressive and should not be considered bad — and they can certainly fit into the definition of real success. Furthermore, the lessons that I shared in this book will in fact help you to achieve these types of accomplishments. But I am saying that **real success goes further and deeper than the worldly proof points of "success" and can even be obtained without achieving the worldly proof points.** The janitor at NASA, my mother, the everyday heroes and friend Amy mentioned in lesson #3, or the fisherman from the fable in the "For What" chapter can all be every bit the story of real success as the professional athlete, CEO, and others recognized throughout this book and in the broader society.

But if you do in fact achieve visible goals and accomplishments, but do so in a way that you neglect helping or rooting for others (i.e. being a great teammate, getting the best of everyone), especially those closest to you, and find yourself self-centered, unfulfilled, anxious, hateful, constantly trying to impress others, and are lacking deep joy, you have not attained real success. If you make it to the pinnacle of your chosen sport or profession, even after overcoming many obstacles, and yet have broken relationships with those closest to you out of selfishness, you have not attained real success. If, for your life, you have not chosen as the "the aim or purpose of what you've set out to accomplish" (the basic definition of success) as being joined with God in heaven someday, I firmly believe that you will never achieve real success.

"Success" in quotations is the definition that never satisfies; its focus is on comparing oneself to other people and on the external measures of success (e.g. income, size of home, material wealth, fame, social media followers, etc.). There is always somebody who has done more, is recognized as more, and has more. This focus can easily drive bad behaviors aimed at obtaining the external measures of "success" instead of fulfilling the internal desire for satisfaction, peace and joy. Real success cuts across all the aspects of your life. So winning in sports or your career, but losing in your family or community does not describe real success.

It took me a long time to get over the level of importance that I placed on athletic achievements and professional "success." Instead of looking at my experiences as tremendous gifts from God, including the losses, professional shortcomings, and personal failures, I held on to the mental state of "coulda shoulda woulda" — what I *could have* done, *should have* done, or *would have* done to achieve even higher levels of "success" in the eyes of the world. This happens to people in just about all sports, careers, and even in families, with self-talk sounding like, "I could have been better in athletics; I should have risen even higher in my company; I would have made more money if...; Our family coulda... shoulda...woulda..."

Only when the light clicked for me and my answer to the "For What?" question cleared the way for me to completely choose God as My Guide was I able to fully embrace real success. I was at the top of my career, working for a great company, making a lot of money, and feeling abundantly blessed with a wonderful family, but still I was anxious about doing more, achieving more, making a bigger mark in the world, and not knowing what I should be doing to feel real success in my life. But after thinking about that "For What?" question deeply for several weeks, I came to the conclusion that I needed to be "all in" for Jesus Christ. I have always had Christ as a part of my life, and even as a "big part" of my life at times, as I have heard people describe their faith, but I don't believe that I had yet chosen Him as THE only driving force of my life, in other words, my Lord. And when I did, I then could absolutely appreciate my own accomplishments and celebrate those of others more authentically. I could see clearly what my next steps in life would be and how I could better serve my family and others. I was also then able to more graciously accept my shortcomings and failures as blessings and was able to accept the same for others, especially those closest to me. I have never felt more fulfilled and joyful in my life.

For you who have already faced and have even overcome tremendous hardships in your lives, weathering terrible storms, and perhaps having way more than your share of misfortune, you can still fall short of real success. Despite overcoming incredible obstacles, you are not guaranteed a happy, fulfilling ending.

But if you answer the door at which Jesus stands knocking and waiting to come into your life, filling you with the Holy Spirit, giving you the inspiration and capability to learn and live all other life lessons and achieve many goals — in other words, if you select God as Your Guide — your real success will be the fruits of that Holy Spirit. These fruits are **love, joy, peace, patience, kindness, goodness, faithfulness, gentleness, and self-control;** and these are the measures of real success which will bring to you a deep fulfillment, peace, and joy beyond any other victories, accomplishments, fame, and fortune.

As Jesus asked his disciples so profoundly in the gospel of Matthew (16:26), *"For what will it profit a man if he gains the whole world and forfeits his soul?"*

Pick Role-Models of Real Success

In this light, I challenge you to pick role models of real success and not only those who have attained professional, financial, or celebrity success. I mentioned some of my professional role-models in Lesson #5: Peak Performance State, and I have mentioned and quoted a several others throughout this book. But even more important to my life than athletic or professional role models are my life role-models, mostly the less-well-known but more powerful influences on my life and real success; including my wife Sue, my mother, my siblings and their spouses, several of my extended family members, my closest and oldest friends, my hometown heroes, and my half-crazy father (for selected attributes only…I say with a smile). Some of my role models have in fact achieved great athletic and professional success, even celebrity status, but most important for all of these are the human beings they've become and the lives they live — best friends, wonderful parents, kind and gentle hearts, joyful and faithful disciples of Christ. They have proven to me that you can in fact have real success, **abundant life** as Jesus calls it, across the board (athletics, career, family, life) and they inspire me and help me to live that way every day. So be sure to define your "success" as **real success** and pick the right role-models.

Visualize Success and Play Backwards

Father John Riccardo, who I've mentioned on a couple occasions in this book, and a success (no quotes) role-model of mine, was a gifted multi-sport athlete in his younger days, and is an even more gifted Catholic priest today. He continues to actively enjoy golf when he can get away from his busy ministry, sometimes for building relationships or simply for personal time to relax. He shared with me a helpful analogy from the game of golf that applies to this concept of achieving real success in the game of life and how one may go about attaining it. Father John described the analogy this way to me:

> *Great athletes have an ability to visualize. This is extremely helpful for real success. The visualization here comes from golf. As you well know, great golfers play golf backwards. Most people who play golf stand at the tee and swing as hard as they can, and then go and try to find the ball. Then, they hit it again and repeat. Finally, they get in on the green and then eventually into the hole and move on. Rory [McIlroy] doesn't play golf that way. Rory, and every other professional golfer, stands at the tee and asks the question, "Where do I need to be on the green to have the best chance to make a birdie (or better). Then, what distance do I want to hit my approach shot from to give me the best chance of being there on the green, and only after that, where do I want to hit my tee shot."*

Life is also best played backwards. People who live life in a truly great way, who reach real success, start by asking the question, "What do I want to hear when (not if!) I die?" Each of us is going to stand at the end of our life before God, the God who created us out of love, rescued us by His cross, and destined us for eternal life. But it's our decision to respond to that offer of eternal life that now matters. And so, we will all either hear, "Well done! Good and faithful servant; enter into the joy of your Master!" or we will hear, "Depart from me, you accursed, into the fire prepared for the evil and his angels." Which one do we want to hear? That's a no-brainer! So, how should we live our lives now so as to make sure that's what He says on that very real day that is going to come for each of us?

Father John certainly has a gift of effectively developing and then communicating life's most important messages — though he would be the first to attribute his words to the Holy Spirit. Such a simple and helpful perspective from the world of sports to apply to The Game of a Lifetime.

Make it Stick

I n the spirit of *Lesson #6: Bias for Action*, now is the time to apply anything you learned from this book, something you want to improve upon. Do something significant right now. Avoid letting this opportunity slip by as one of those great ideas and good intentions that never amounted to anything beyond reading a book.

There are an infinite number of ways you can go about committing to, adopting, growing, and becoming highly skilled in any or all of these 9 Lessons starting today. I offer you three approaches to help you craft the approach that works best for you.

Film Session Reviews

Patterned after a film session review the day after playing a game in sports, you'll see in Appendix I two sample Film Session Scorecards for you to consider using as follows:

a) Select the lesson(s) you've chosen to adopt. I recommend eventually selecting all 9 lessons, but you may want to begin with a few and then add others as you start to see consistent improvement, lesson by lesson.

b) Select your frequency of "watching film." I recommend weekly or every two weeks, at least initially, to have ample reviews of where you're getting better or getting worse. Step away from your daily grind and evaluate how you've performed in the areas you've targeted for improvement and growth.

c) For each of the targeted areas for improvement/growth, give yourself a "+" (got better or did well) or a "-" (got worse or did nothing) since the time of your last film session. There is no such thing as staying the same. You either got better with tangible evidence to prove it or you got worse due to no practice and/or no evidence of improvement.

d) Establish a goal for total pluses (+) minus total minuses (-) for each review session and, over time, increase your total goal.

e) Track your progress. Adjust your approach as required to achieve your desired level of performance (your goal).

Note: A leader of a team or coach can develop a summary score card with the exact same layout for aggregate scores of all individual assessments in order to track team progress.

Mentoring or coaching sessions with role models and experts

Consider identifying a role model or mentor for the targeted lessons that you're committed to adopt and improve. You may select one person or multiple, depending on their expertise and their ability to help you with your improvements over time. You may use existing coaches, spiritual leaders, parents, siblings, etc. Ask their permission to periodically sit with you to talk about your goals, plans, and how they can help provide you feedback to improve. You may wish to use the Film Session Scorecard as a tool to aid you and them in your discussions.

Journaling

Consider a daily or weekly journal to write down your goals, progress, challenges, plans, and observations along your journey to improve. Journaling is an effective way to force yourself to stop and reflect on how it is going. Actually writing down your thoughts is often a helpful exercise to clarify thinking, be it on assessing performance, developing improvement plans, highlighting issues, and working through struggles. Again, journaling can be used to support more effective coaching or mentoring sessions and can be used in conjunction with the scorecard idea.

These are only three approaches to "making it stick." These may work for you or not. What matters is whatever approach works for you.

Assess the Journey

My mother-in-law Marge gave me a little gift in the first year that I knew her, which sat on my desk at work for over 28 years. It was a simple paper weight with an engraving that said, "Success is a journey, not a destination." I found it to be an important daily reminder as I was striving toward success, a reminder not to think about success as some target way down the road, but instead to consider every day and every moment an opportunity to be successful.

Whatever your approach to making these or other habits stick in your life, assess the journey of success, not the destination.

Final Thoughts and Closing Prayer

I've written this book to help young people (and everybody else) experience the abundance that I have been able to simply taste in my life and yet am overwhelmed with joy — and I know that there is more where that came from. I am confident that the 9 Lessons in this book can help people of all ages achieve more success in their lives, real success.

I have often learned the hard way as to what does not bring joy and fulfillment. However, I know that God has blessed me beyond my most hopeful dreams in knowing Him. And in knowing Jesus Christ as my Savior, I am able to hear Him as the Lord of my life, with His Holy Spirit directing my decisions and actions. He gave me the tremendous opportunity to play athletics to be used as a foundation for the remainder of my life. He allowed me to have the thrill of success, the misery of failure, and everything in-between at a young age so that I could leverage those lessons to achieve success in my working career and family life. He gave me the gifts of success and failure on earth, but most importantly, He showed me the missing link between "success" and real success in my life and I believe He wants me to share that with others, especially young people who are traveling a similar road that I began a half-century ago.

With this in mind, I say to you young athletes. No matter how long you will play football, basketball, volleyball, softball, baseball, hockey, or whatever sport or activity you choose, whether you play one more season, a few more years, play in college, or even professionally, or if your athletic career is over, *be completely aware of the life lessons you are learning and the life skills you are developing right now, or have recently experienced and learned.* Take advantage of every minute of the fantastic opportunity called athletics. Maximize to the fullest your sport(s) as a training ground to achieve real success in your family, career, and life.

And for you who have not chosen athletics as part of your journey, be completely aware of the life lessons you are learning in your own selected activities, those that challenge you to: be coachable, be a great teammate, do your job well, master adversity, maintain peak performance state, have a bias for action, develop discipline as a habit, and get the best of everyone.

Closing Prayer

I pray that after we've all thrown our last pass, scored our last points, netted the last goal, made that final big block, received our last paycheck, and said goodbye to our family and friends, we are able to say,

"I have fought the good fight, I have finished the race, I have kept the faith. Now there is in store for me the crown of righteousness, which the Lord, the righteous Judge, will award to me on that day—and not only to me, but also to all who have longed for his appearing." *(2 Timothy 4: 7-8)*

And after you win that Game of a Lifetime, when Success (in the eyes of God) beats "Success" (in the eyes of the world), and you are in that locker room in heaven, along with all of the teammates you brought with you, **oh what a celebration it will be!!!**

Congratulations on finishing this book! Doing so is an example of living several of these lessons. You are on your way to a more profoundly successful, fulfilling, and joyful life.

God bless you and **thank you** for giving me this privilege of sharing these life lessons with you.

Appendix I

Sample Film Session Scorecards

Film Session Scorecard

Lesson #	Lesson Title (Area of Focus)	Priority Now?	June 5th	June 19th	July 2nd	(Date of Session)	(Date of Session)	(Date of Session)	(Date of Session)	(Date of Session)	(Date of Session)
1	Be Coachable	Yes	+	+	+						
2	Be a Great Teammate	Yes	+	+	+						
3	Play Your Position Well	Yes	+	+	+						
4	Master Adversity	Yes	-	-	+						
5a	Peak Performance State - Mental	Yes	-	-	-						
5b	Peak Performance State - Physical	Yes	+	+	+						
5c	Peak Performance State - Emotional	Yes	+	+	+						
6	Bias for Action	Yes	+	+	+						
7	Discipline as a Habit	Yes	-	-	+						
8	Get the Best of Everybody	Yes	+	-	+						
9	God as Your Guide	Yes	+	+	-						
	Total Pluses Less Minuses		5	3	7						
	Goal		5	5	5	6	6	6	7	7	8

"+" means getting better or doing well, with evidence/examples of doing well

"-" means getting worse, not doing well, or doing nothing (doing nothing is getting worse)

Observations/Highlights/Concerns

Film Session Scorecard

Date of Film Session	GOAL Total "+" Less "-"	ACTUAL Total "+" Less "-"	Be Coachable	Be a Great Teammate	Play Your Position Well	Master Adversity	Peak Performance State - Mental	Peak Performance State - Physical	Peak Performance State - Emotional	Bias for Action	Discipline as a Habit	Get the Best of Everybody	God as Your Guide	Evidence Highlights Observations
5/6	5		+	+	-	-	-	+	+	+	-	+		Taking feedback well
5/19	5	5	+	-	-	+	+	+	+	+	-	+		Great eh and run
6/2	5	6	+-	+-	-	+	+	+	-	+	+	-	+	Still learning new position
6/16	5													
6/30	5													
7/14	5													
7/28	6													
8/11	6													
8/25	6													
9/8	6													
9/22	6													
10/6	6													
10/20	7													
11/3	7													
11/17	7													
12/1	7													
12/15	7													
12/29	7													
1/12	8													
1/26	8													

"+" means getting better or doing well, with evidence/examples of doing well

"-" means getting worse, not doing well, or doing nothing significant (doing nothing means getting worse)

Made in the USA
Columbia, SC
17 October 2020